TOOLS FOR THE TODDLER YEARS

Yvonne Gustafson, Ph.D
and Kendra Hovey

Illustrated by Greg Bonnell

To my family—treasured husband and children, Bob, Amanda, and Andrew; two brothers; six sisters; plus extended family both present and remembered who through our shared lives have mirrored, echoed, and expanded my capacity to love.

—*Yvonne*

To Cleo

—*Kendra*

Design and Illustrations Greg Bonnell

Printed in the United States of America

First Printing, 2014

ISBN 978-0-9903462-0-3

your-parenting-matters.com

CONTENTS

INTRODUCTION

You have a wonderfully active and exploring toddler underfoot. You have giggles and hugs, but also meltdowns and tears. You have refusals, spaghetti dumped on the floor, maybe even, spaghetti dumped on the cat. And while every day you navigate the bumpy terrain of eating, sleeping, the car seat, transitioning, diapering, playing, protesting, and sharing, questions may loop around your head: *Is he stimulated enough? Too much? Eating too much? Not enough? Is she making eye contact? Is THAT normal? And, the ever present, constant concern—Am I doing the right thing? Am I a good parent?*

Like everyone, you have questions and you have challenges. But with life running at a toddler's pace, odds are you barely have a moment to think, let alone read. We know you don't need a book you *have to make time for,* so we made this book *for the time you have.* It is designed to fit seamlessly into the multi-tasking, mobile, always interrupted, time-crunched life of a toddler's parent, who—though highly literate—has precious little time to read.

IN THIS BOOK:

- We don't just share advice; we walk you through it. We connect it to developmental whys and hows, and stay attentive to parental stressors, needs, and overall family dynamics.

- We focus on exactly the behaviors that most perplex and exhaust parents of toddlers.

- We provide sensible tools and strategies that are easy-to-find, easy-to-recall, clear, succinct, and demonstrated in-practice with illustrations and sample scripts.

- We ready you for the day-to-day challenges, so that day-to-day you can also experience the joy in parenting and feel capable, loving, and confident as you, in turn, nurture a capable, loving, and confident child.

HOW TO READ THIS BOOK

If you were to begin on page one, you'd learn, first, about the physical, emotional, and developmental life of the toddler and then, in chapter two, about the physical and emotional life of you, the parent or caregiver of a toddler.

Next, you'd come to colorful **Part II: Glance & Go Guides**, which offers swift help with the most intense toddler behaviors (think, meltdowns), and then on to our concise guides to common, but less urgent, toddler topics in **Part III: Easing the Everyday**.

But, *if* you are reaching for this book because you have a question, forget page one. You'll get to it. Right now let your question tell you where to start. For instance, if it begins:

What do I do when...??!!

Skip straight to **Part II** (p. 30) and get the glance-and-go help you need for meltdowns, hitting, kicking, biting, grabbing, whining, rigid refusing bodies, floppy boneless protesting bodies, and other physically exhausting, emotionally stressful, but developmentally normal, toddler behaviors.

Why does my toddler...?

Begin at the beginning. In chapter one, *The Hard-Working Toddler* (p. 7) you'll get the developmental explanation behind why your toddler spins until dizzy, for example, or insists on climbing up the slide or shifts quickly from calm to explosive or can't sleep without his lovey. You'll understand not just what is going on inside developmentally and physiologically, but what it looks like, behaviorally, on the outside—an insight that can strengthen empathy, diffuse anger and blame, and allow parental expectations to better match a child's ability.

Why am I feeling...?

Open first to *The Hard-Working Parent* on page 19. Here you will find support as well as information about the skilled work that parents do on a daily basis, and also ***the much less talked about* emotional work of coming to know oneself as a mom or dad.** This chapter can help you understand why you are experiencing certain disruptive feelings, and also how to lessen and manage them.

How can I support my toddler with...?

If it concerns an explosive behavior, such as meltdowns, hitting, and mega-resistance, go to **Part II**. Otherwise, **Part III: Easing the Everyday** (p. 50) is where you'll find concise guides to big issue topics, such as, how to support sleep, improve nutrition, identify potty readiness, handle "sharing," have a playdate that doesn't end in a meltdown, and manage the daily tasks of life with a busy toddler underfoot.

No matter the page you turn to first, you should read every page with an understanding of the philosophy (see p. 4) that informs every bit of advice in this book.

And, please always check our advice, and all advice, against the wisdom of the best expert on your child—you.

1. Listen to the expert—you

There is no secret, no special trick. As inviting as a parenting formula may be, always be skeptical of one-stop solutions. Parenting is an art, practiced by you, supported by others—family, friends, parenting books, and, we hope, this parenting book. So if you're looking for an expert on your child, you've already found it—you.

Because of your hands-on care, you will know best if your child responds to singing (*"Let's get in the car so we can sing the car seat song!"*) or if she loves ritual, silliness, or the very concrete message of a chart or timer. Parental intuition is not to be ignored. [But, if you feel yours has been disrupted by a difficult childhood or trauma, it helps to have a trusted individual who can listen long enough for you to find clarity.]

2. Get to know the expert

Along with understanding your child, understanding yourself is an important element of parenting (p. 19). It will also help you to make the best use of the help offered in a parenting book. For instance, a person who tends towards a more indulgent parenting style might understand the parenting tool "acknowledgement of hard work" (pg. 37) quite differently from someone more familiar with a rigid style. One parental lens takes it as an endorsement of bribery. Another sees coddling. Understanding that the personal lens exists, makes it possible to see the tool for what it is—a simple reminder about cause & effect and motivation, both key to human activity at any age.

3. Make it a conversation

Many of us have a tendency to think of books as a definitive source. We suggest that you think of the parenting book more like you would a friend. You rely on your friends for ideas, support, understanding, and the best knowledge they can share, but you do not expect your friends to have all the answers or for their answers to be right for you all of the time. The parenting book is one voice, a valued and knowledgeable voice (or it should be), but still one voice in a bigger conversation.

4. Choose your friends wisely

"Consider the source" is an especially useful adage as you decide what written support is best for you and your family. Because parenting is such a complex task, many respected fields of study contribute to the pool of information and advice. Physicians bring a focus on health; psychologists bring an emphasis on relationship-building; neuroscientists and child development researchers bring attention to change, growth, and milestones; and it's not only faith-based authors who frame parenting within a set a beliefs, every author brings personal and professional values to his or her work, including us (see p. 4).

5. Do a gut check

Always test advice against your own intuition and values. Take for example two kinds of advice you may have been given about infant sleep: *Crying to sleep is an effective sleep strategy* vs. *Meet your baby's needs so he doesn't cry*. Sometimes, when using the cry-it-out strategy, mom is crying harder than baby. For this mom, the cry-it-out strategy is probably not a good fit for the family right now. It may be that at an intuitive level she is reading a different need for her child or that she does not yet fully believe her child to be ready for this developmental demand.

When the strategy does not fit the parent's values it is much harder to follow-through and it is, therefore, much less likely to work. But, even if it did work, it would do little to support the parent self-confidence that will be needed to face the next parenting challenge.

APPROACH & PHILOSOPHY

This book is centered in the understanding that parenting with respect, affection, and support makes kids feel confident and loved, and makes parents feel successful and loving. We have no trademark for our philosophy, nor do we align ourselves with any other. Our approach is based on the understanding that, no matter the latest craze, parenting is always about warmth and control, and our advice, tools, and strategies seek a balance of these two so that the child feels nurtured, secure and loved (warmth) as well as valued and listened to, while given clear boundaries and appropriate expectations (control).

This is an approach shared by many. It is supported by solid research in psychology and parent education, and it is reflected in the lived-wisdom of many from past generations. It has also been illustrated, charted, and graphed—*many times over*. You'll find our version on page 28, which in four quadrants illustrates four different ways of balancing warmth and control. Below, we've sliced off a piece of that chart—the top right—to further demonstrate the quadrant in which we base our parenting help:

Authoritative/Democratic

POSSIBLE BELIEF SYSTEM:
Everyone in this family counts. My job is to love, coach, and guide.

WHAT IT CAN LOOK LIKE AT THIS AGE:
- Free cuddles & smiles
- Rhythm to the day
- Acknowledgement rather than praise: *I see you climbing the slide ladder, are you proud?*
- Collaborating with the child to problem solve (not abdicating to the child)

PARENT CAN BE:
- Firm, but not rigid
- Respectful
- Cooperative
- Loving

Everything in this book is also based in the following five beliefs:

❶ We believe parenting is an art, practiced by you, and supported by the wisdom and research of others. There is no one-size-fits-all solution.

❷ We believe parenting is joyful serious stuff. It's an important job, as we often hear. But, as we very rarely hear, it's also an interesting job. Nurturing children is inherently impactful; it is wondrously complex, fascinating, and can be fun.

❸ We believe your toddler is a human being. Not an alien. Not a caveman. Not a biter. Not a screamer. Not a label at all, and not a caricature.

❹ We believe you are a smart and capable person looking for parenting support you can trust in a format you can use. Our mission is to supply you with solid information, concrete strategies and tools, insights into child development, and a nudge to frame the problems you face in a positive way, so that you can feel supported in the hard and important work you are doing and build unique solutions that work for you, your family, and the special, fully-faceted, complex human being that is your child.

❺ We believe this is a book. It is not your best friend and it will not pretend to be, nor will it pretend to be an infallible doctor. It's not. No one is.

LANGUAGE & OTHER PRACTICALITIES

- In these pages, the toddler is sometimes a he, sometimes a she. We tried our best to randomly alternate between genders.

- Parents are sometimes mom, sometimes dad, but more often mom. Though we firmly believe in men's equal participation in parenting, the reality is women, by a huge margin, do more of the work of parenting. It feels only right to acknowledge this work.

- Though we trust that it is obvious, we state it here nonetheless: There is nothing in this book that can be used to justify any kind or type of harmful, abusive, disrespectful, neglectful, or dangerously indulgent acts.

We've tailor-made this book for your specific needs as a parent or caregiver of a toddler. We hope that it provides you with tools and strategies, as well as a deeper developmental understanding of your impressively busy toddler. We hope, too, that you feel our respect and support for the physical, emotional, and spiritual stamina it takes for you to do the best you can for your toddler, your family, and yourself.

PART I: YOUR TODDLER AND YOU

THE HARD-WORKING TODDLER

Imagine waking up to a new day—a day so new that you don't know what comes next. You have no schedule, no timeline, in fact, you don't even know what this thing called "time" is. You are so unable to plan ahead that it doesn't even occur to you to get dressed, brush your teeth, or even eat breakfast. Instead you react. Without being able to predict it or plan for it, you feel hunger (perhaps mightily) and want food (now!). You are, literally, living in the moment.

If you can imagine this day, then you know what every day is like for the toddler. As adults, we *can only imagine* what this day is like, we can't experience it. Our fully developed brains simply won't let us. We have no OFF switch for time or for planning, categorizing, structuring, and predicting. And, just as we can't turn all this stuff off, the toddler can't turn it on.

Nor can we "lose ourselves" in quite the way a toddler can. When was the last time you confused your physical body with another? Yet the toddler can feel *I want blanket* and fully expect your arms to then provide it. In the young brain, the boundaries between self and others are still a bit fuzzy. The experts call this state "*enmeshment*."

Clearly, there is much that is different between a toddler and an adult. But there is also much that is the same. Imagine, for instance, that the absolute foundation of your existence is love. The experts call this state "*attachment*," but whatever it's called, both toddler and adult know exactly what it is and how it feels.

The Toddler is Not a Small Adult

We say this as a reminder of developmental differences, but what else does it mean?

It means you can stop worrying.

Every parent wonders who their child will be and how they will grow, sometimes we do this too much—projecting current behavior into the future.

You don't expect your two-year-old to go off to college in diapers, so there is no reason to believe a meltdown at age three means you'll have a teenager who throws tantrums.

A lack of focus in your toddler is not itself a sign of Attention Deficit Disorder.

And, a refusal to share a toy now does not necessarily say anything about how generous your child will be at 5, 10, 15, 25, 50, or 100. While a child is a toddler, it's okay to act like a toddler.

It may sound like a contradiction—You and your toddler are different; You and your toddler are the same—but understanding the truth of both these statements is an important part of parenting. *Toddlers are not small adults.* Yet, the toddler's needs, desires, struggles, and motivations are not unlike our own. Different developmental stages may make us uniquely different, but we are each fully human.

Of course, in the throes of parenting it is easy to lose sight of this understanding—not just because of the stress of the moment, but because of two important realities:

- The abilities adults rely on the most, such as time, memory, order, and prediction, are so automatic and easy for us that we can forget that these same abilities are *physiologically impossible* for the toddler.

- Toddler behavior and emotions are expressed so intensely and so physically, **the reason behind the behavior is often buried in a deluge of wails, whines, foot-stomping, and tears.** When we can identify the emotion underlying the behavior, we can empathize with the toddler's strongest needs and wants: to be fed, secure, warm, comforted, and loved—and even the toddler's primary struggle, the desire for independence and control that pushes right up against a fear of independence and control. The hard part is seeing through the storm to these underlying needs, wants, and struggles.

That's why in this book, whenever we discuss toddler physiology and development we *connect it to behavior.* In other words, we explain not just what it is, but what it looks like.

What we know about the toddler from research, as well as from generation upon generation of parents and caregivers, could fill volumes. This is the short version, and it is organized (after all, the adult brain does love to categorize!) into three overlapping sections: The Brain, The Body, and The Heart.

THE BRAIN

THE TODDLER BRAIN IS BUSY

It has twice as many cells as the adult brain.
Babies are born with as many cells in their brains as there are stars in the Milky Way—somewhere around 100 billion. The brain will create and strengthen some connections through learning and practice and prune others, gradually and continually creating an organized structure within which to place larger and larger chunks of content.

The toddler brain is twice as active as the adult brain.
As the toddler experiences life, her brain is hard at work learning and making complex associations. For instance, the toddler looks at a flat, inert picture of a black and white shape on a page and she knows it is a cow. She hears the sound "moo" and again she knows: cow. She sees a lumbering, smelly, cod-chewing animal on the other side of the fence and, again, she gets it: cow.

The pre-verbal child routinely translates from a two-dimensional world to a three-dimensional world—a moving, unpredictable, and textured three-dimensional world at that. The toddler is performing amazing cognitive feats like this all the time as she works hard to negotiate and understand the complicated maze of life. **As adults, it is sometimes hard for us to see the toddler's hard work because, to us, it looks like play.**

The toddler brain is acquiring language at an amazing pace.
Researchers believe that the human brain acquires around 40 new words a day during the 2nd and 3rd years of life. Receptive language comes first. This means the young child can understand and act on words he hears long before he can speak them.

A Quick Note About *Your* Toddler

In this chapter we draw a picture of how the toddler experiences the world, but we understand you are especially interested in how *your* toddler experiences the world.

After all, he or she is an absolutely unique being, and from day one you have been discovering who this wondrous new child is—personality, temperament, likes, dislikes, charms, quirks, and needs.

Yet, it is also true that the parameters of what a child can do and think are linked to physiological development.

We believe your expert understanding of your own child working in tandem with an understanding of age-based developmental abilities is a perfect combination for nurturing and guiding your child as he or she grows, learns, and thrives.

To sleep is to learn. Sleep is not a time for this very busy brain "to rest," as we typically understand it, but to solidify the new connections and organize the structure for new learning.

THE TODDLER "SEES" EVERYTHING
The toddler brain is open and receptive.

The adult brain is constantly and unconsciously prioritizing information and weeding out distractions. The toddler brain does not have these same blinders.

Though research suggests that the young brain is primed to be especially responsive to certain types of information—those that encourage language development and emotional connection, for instance—the young brain is open and, like a sponge, soaks everything in.

This is how we grow and learn, but it brings with it challenges. **With so much to see and absorb, the day can get overwhelming and exhausting.**

The simple experience of entering a new place—a friend's house for a playgroup, for instance—can present an absolute explosion of stimuli for a toddler. There are toys of different shapes and colors, moving children, big adults, a new wallpaper calling out to be touched, a cat curled up on a pillow, a sudden "glub-glub–glub" coming from the aquarium, and the glow of a computer screen in the corner.

While the adult automatically catalogs all this stimuli and easily hones in on a focus, the toddler cannot. So with all this and more going on, it may be hard for a toddler to just "go and play."

Even if you know she will have fun, even if she wants to be there, she may need time and support when entering new places.

THE TODDLER LIVES IN THE MOMENT
The toddler has not developed an understanding of time.

An understanding of time allows us to consciously learn from the past and to anticipate the future. It enables us to keep sequential elements in our heads at the same time.

The toddler brain does not have this same understanding of time, and as a result:

- **"Later "and "two minutes" are meaningless to the toddler.** They need concrete and experiential markers such as "after nap" or "when daddy comes home" instead.

- **The toddler does not understand the trajectory of the day.** He does not have an internal awareness of the flow of morning into day into night and all the things that happen along the way.

  This means he does not anticipate hunger. This means that when a parent leaves in the morning, he does not have a sense of when in his life that parent will return. It is easy to see, then, how the lack of understanding and control, and the suddenness of physical drives can result in frustration or crankiness. Parents and caregivers create anchors within the chaos by continually narrating the story of the day:

  > ...We are done with breakfast. Now we will get coats and get in the car and I'll take you to grandma's house.

  So as not to overwhelm, the story should be restricted to two or three elements at a time. Rituals and traditions, such as a piggyback up to bed or a carseat song for getting in the car, can also help bring order to the inherent chaos of the toddler's day.

- **The toddler cannot multitask or hold multiple steps in her head at once**. This is why it is best to limit choices to two—"oatmeal or egg?" "Tennis shoes or sandals?"—and why toddlers do best when given one step at a time to accomplish a task. This is also why you will find yourself repeating instructions over and over again.

- **The toddler cannot necessarily make the connection "I'll do this because it will lead to that."** So toddlers often show resistance to things that they *want to* do. For instance, a toddler may refuse to put shoes on even though shoes are needed to go to the much-loved park.

Toddlers can also easily become frustrated as they become part of a timeline of activity that they do not understand, even if it is activity they enjoy. Again, narrating (and repeating) the connections between the task and the resulting activity and narrating (and repeating) the course of events can help to ease these kinds of transitions.

- **For the toddler it is very hard work to wait.** Because he lives in the present moment, everything that is happening now is all there is. He cannot on his own initiative look forward to what will come after the wait, nor comprehend the necessity of the wait.

Yet waiting is a part of life, and the toddler should not be exempt from learning this skill. He will simply need extra support. Songs, distractions, and talking with the child during the process of waiting are some great ways to help.

THE TODDLER IS A CONCRETE THINKER
The toddler brain does not yet have a fully developed cerebral cortex (where abstract thought is centered). The toddler is a literal thinker and understands best when words are concrete and specific. This is why visual aids, such as charts and calendars, are often helpful (you may remember using tools like paper chains or advent calendars while waiting anxiously for a holiday).

The toddler learns by doing. Rather than watch and then understand that the ball is too big for the hole, she must try to put the big ball in the small hole. She will pour the contents of a bucket into a cup because she can't predict that it won't fit.

The puzzle piece doesn't fit? Time for the toddler to pull out her go-to problem-solving skill: *Push harder!*

Just because all this behavior is normal doesn't mean it's not frustrating for parents.

Awareness of where that frustration can take us (ex: an angry *"If you don't put the shoe on then we won't go play!"*) and having an alternative on hand (ex: a more patient *"When your shoes are on then we can go play"*) can help us to face that challenge successfully.

THE BODY

THE TODDLER EXPERIENCES THE WORLD WITH HER WHOLE BODY

To build connections between her billions of neurons she needs "input" from her senses.

We are born with a neural framework. Everything we experience, touch, smell, eat, feel, and hear fills in the framework. But more than just filling, this stuff of life is building and rebuilding the neural network, forming new pathways and connections.

Thus, the toddler is primed to learn and is developmentally driven to engage with the world using her whole body and each one of her senses. The toddler will push, grab, squeeze, roll, lick, taste; **she will engage her whole body to discover and understand the world.** This is why the toy may go in the mouth, why the food might get squished between the fingers before it is tasted, and why the bowl of pasta might also go on the head—*it holds my food but is it a hat, too?*—and, as every parent is well aware, this is why we keep a watchful eye. If the toddler is awake, the parent is on duty!
[More on that in chapter two: *The Hard-Working Parent.*]

He cannot always control his body, but he absolutely needs to use it.

Why do some kids love to make themselves dizzy, or have daddy "swing me one more time?" Because it's really fun! It also helps them learn to control their bodies. The toddler needs to practice balance and spatial orientation. The body needs to stimulate its vestibular system (balance and posture) and proprioceptive sense (orientation of the body in space).

Thus, it's quite normal and common for the toddler to run in circles until he falls down dizzy and to hold on to the armrest of the couch and jump up and down, up and down, up and down, endlessly. The

The tools and toys of toddler play need to be durable. Caregivers should inspect them regularly for broken edges, loose pieces, or other possible hazards.

toddler will very likely try to run and climb up the slide instead of using the ladder. It's not just that he doesn't know or doesn't remember the rule about the slide. It's that he has these big leg muscles to use and an inner ear to orient to the slant. It looks like play—and it is play—but it is also important work.

The toddler has big muscle work to do and small muscle work to do.
It is not only the legs that run and the arms that throw (gross motor/big muscle) that are developing, but also the fingers that grasp and the mouth that sips and the tongue that helps make sounds (fine motor/small muscle). In fact, the tiny, detailed movements that usually require hand-eye coordination are just as tough and usually tougher than big muscle work.

That it takes longer (and lots of practice) to develop the control and precision needed to master these fine motor skills is so clearly reflected in speech development. For example, a child may easily understand a directive such as, "*Go find your shoes*" but may be several weeks away from speaking words that adults can recognize.

Likewise, pulling off shoes typically comes long before pulling on socks, or managing something as complicated as buttons.

THE TODDLER'S THOUGHTS AND BODY WORK IN UNISON
His instantaneous experience of the world means there's no real separation between thinking and doing.
The adult brain can mull, consider, mentally rehearse, and engage in idle thoughts. But for the toddler there is no such thing as an idle thought. **The moment the toddler's interest is captured, the body is already moving toward it.**

This meshing of the mind and the body means, for example, that no sooner does the toddler see the cat than she has him by the tail. It also means that a twinge of new teeth felt in the mouth can easily become a sudden chomp. And because seeing and moving are so integrated, young bodies will often follow their eyes, literally, so that they go head first down the slide or down the stairs.

THE TODDLER CANNOT PREDICT INJURY TO HERSELF OR TO OTHERS

She is only beginning to understand cause and effect, and also how to control her constantly changing body. Toddlers can seem fearless: They will walk into the path of a moving swing. They will crash their toy cart into another's toy cart. They will run right up to a strange dog. **But they are not so much fearless as they are counting on you to keep them safe.** This is something they are unable to do for themselves. They can't yet predict what will hurt them, nor can they predict what will hurt others.

At the same time, it is hard for them to moderate their bodies and to control hard and soft touching. Thus, it is common for a touch meant as a *pat-pat-pat t*o come out as a *whomp-whomp-whomp*. We can help by keeping our toddlers safe and also by demonstrating and modeling over and over again (for instance, "*kitty likes a soft touch,*" we say, as we glide the child's hand softly over the cat's back).

THE TODDLER BODY CAN MELTDOWN WHEN UNDER STRESS

His central nervous system is not fully developed. Because of this, it can become overloaded and crash. Hunger, tiredness, too much stimuli, discomfort, and frustration are common loads that can build until the body crashes. Often, the limbs will flail and the body will flop to the floor. The back may also arch: This is literally tension of the central nervous system, which is located in the spine. **Once underway, a meltdown is a biological response, not a willful action.** The child can't make it stop, but has to work hard to regain control of his body.

[See Glance & Go Guides: Meltdowns on p. 31.]

The toddler is working to integrate all her muscles. Over several months she will be able to manage the difference between light pats and more intense touch.

Flight, fight, freeze are human survival reactions. As we mature we learn when to run from a fear, when to fight to protect ourselves, and when to pause and think before reacting.

THE TODDLER CANNOT REGULATE EMOTIONS
Emotional maturity is learned and *physiological.*
The toddler has BIG emotions. When she is happy, she is really happy. When she is sad, she is really sad. The area of the brain responsible for regulation of the emotions is still developing. She cannot check, govern, manage, or reason with her emotions, and she cannot be talked out of her emotions.

This is one reason why this age is not the developmental time to force a child to face her fears. A state of sustained or overwhelming fear is a state in which a child not only feels uncomfortable in her world, but also one in which she cannot learn. So if Santa is scary this year, that's okay. Don't force her to sit in his lap, that's something she might be able to do next year or the year after.

LOVE AND ATTACHMENT ARE EVERYTHING
It's "out of sight out of mind"—unless it's attachment.
"We do not live by bread alone." Though seemingly self-evident, this bit of human wisdom has also been confirmed by science. Even if given adequate physical care, we do not thrive healthfully without emotional care. Attachment is the constant grounding element of the toddler's life.

We described earlier how the young brain is physiologically unable to recall the past—put almost any toy away and for the toddler it is truly "out of sight out of mind"—but, **interestingly and mysteriously, love and attachment transcend this physiological system.** Put a "lovey" away and the young child will remember it and miss it. Attachment (and the most important attachment is to the child's primary caretakers) is the foundation and the essence of the toddler's life. Attachment makes his world work.

16

There are wonderful and frustrating moments for the toddler as the struggle for *affective permanence* (you and our relationship exist even when I don't see you) develops and matures. You probably remember when your child learned *object permanence* as an infant (the object exists even when I don't see it) as she delighted in the game of finding the toy under the blanket. Playing peek-a-boo (*mom is gone and here she is!*) is a surprise and delight every time mom is back because *object* but also *affective* permanence is beginning to develop.

As a toddler, there will be cycles/periods in which practicing affective permanence will be difficult, and while the toddler is struggling with this concept of "mom/dad exists even if I don't see her/him," leaving her with a sitter can sometimes be very hard for both parent and child.

A TODDLER'S BOUNDARIES ARE FUZZY
Understanding of the "separate self" is still developing.
In some ways, your toddler is still like the infant who does not differentiate the self from anything else, straddling the state of enmeshment and separateness (*I am me...you are you...but only sort of...*).

When the toddler reaches for what he wants and mom provides it, the toddler's understanding is moving closer to "Mom gets it for me," but still there is the sense of "Mom *is* me"—as if mom is an extension of the child's arm.

Since birth, his caretakers have been the magic that makes his world work. Now the toddler must use different and new tools—sounds and words—to signal his needs and wants, and his caretakers can't or won't always respond right away or how he wants them to. This is new for the toddler and can sometimes be hard.

The other side of this is that the toddler, in coming to understand his separateness, is also coming to understand "No." Toddlers love to experiment with this new idea, sometimes completely confusing their caretakers by throwing out a "No!" even in response to something that they really, really want!

THE TODDLER LOVES TO BE WITH SAME-SIZED PEOPLE

But doesn't always know how to be with same-sized people.

Typically, toddlers enjoy being together, playing side-by-side, making eye contact, smiling, and sometimes echoing each other's play. They engage in parallel play. But they do not yet have the communication skills needed to collaborate with, or to interpret the intent of, another child.

The next stage, interactive or collaborative play between children, requires an ability to negotiate, to follow rules, and to understand and interpret not just words but actions. Toddlers are developing these skills, but **at this point they still need you close by to help them to understand how to be with other children.**

[See the Playdate Guide on p. 67.]

THE TODDLER HAS A UNIQUE RELATIONSHIP WITH OBJECTS

Objects, such as toys, are important to the toddler's understanding of the world.

A toddler hands a toy (a rock, a key, etc) to an adult. The adult often names the object and says "thank you." The toddler waits or soon returns to the adult and puts out her hand. The adult then understands to give the toy back.

Do you know this game? It is repeated millions of times over between adults and young children everywhere (and children may be deeply surprised when they attempt to play this game with other children, who don't know to play by the adult rules). So, what is this game about? Many things. It is about language development, including the communication loop of give-and-take, and it is about the way in which interacting with adults is different than interacting with other toddlers.

This game also serves as an example of the important role that objects play in the toddler's life. The toddler's relationship to objects is different from the adult's relationship with objects. While it is easy for us to confuse a toddler's attachment to things as selfishness or materialism, those are adult interpretations. For the toddler, **objects are developmental tools used to learn and to communicate.** They are tools used to understand the self and others and the relationship between the two.

There is so much more to the toddler than could ever fit in one chapter, and researchers are continually adding to our scientific understanding—sometimes only confirming what parents and caregivers already know—but it is certainly clear that our toddlers are busy at work.

So go ahead and feel proud of that impressive and amazing child in your life. You have every reason to.

THE HARD-WORKING PARENT

Why is this so hard?

When parents ask this question, often they are really asking, "Why is this so hard *for me*?"

Despite the simple truth that parenting *is* hard and that it is hard for *everyone*, many of us can't let go of the belief that it *should* be easier and that it *should* be more fun and that, if it isn't, we have only ourselves to blame.

Why do so many of us feel this way? One reason: **the pressure to be a perfect parent is strong while opportunities to learn and gain experience with young children, parenting, and family-life are at an all-time low.** Set a high bar and offer little support and anyone will feel as if they don't measure up.

But there is another reason, and it's one we don't talk about as much: To be entrusted with the life of another is an enormous responsibility. It is important to acknowledge that, in all honesty, for those who do it best, a bit of self-scrutiny is built into the job.

When we become the "boss" of our children, we also become the "boss" of ourselves, and while our children certainly benefit from our continuing evaluation of our own job performance, no one benefits from an evaluation that is unfair.

Because your dedicated and well-intended "inner boss" may also be demanding and harbor expectations way out of line with reality, we suggest that your "inner boss" quickly review some of the very basic demands and duties of the job:

WANTED: PARENT IN 21ST CENTURY AMERICA

Primary Responsibility:
Ensure the survival, growth, and nurturance of another human being(s).

Hours:
Non-stop. You may get an occasional physical break, subject to interruption at any time, but expect to permanently devote a large chunk of your brain space and emotional energy to the well being of your child.

Duties:
At any given moment, must be ready to be one or more of the following:

nurse, coach, police officer, artist, security guard, sleep consultant, game designer, counselor, doctor, nutritionist, performer (a deep repertoire of rhyming songs preferred), diagnostician, teacher (of math, science, language, health, and, well, everything), policy maker, publicist, mediator, chef, and more.

Additional Duties:
You will continue to be responsible for any and all duties performed prior to the start of this job, including, if relevant, your 40-hour work week, home maintenance, and the on-going nurturance of all other primary relationships.

Required Skills:
- Must be "on your toes" as you will be expected to constantly monitor, calibrate, and predict safety, mood, hunger, tiredness, and more.

- Must try to remain calm even while physically exhausted, sleep deprived and/or pushed to the extreme ends of your emotional spectrum.

- Must be able to "learn on the job" with no instruction or support (though, if time allows, you are welcome to seek these out on your own—*good luck!*)

- Must understand "little eyes are watching you" and learning from you all the time.

- Must be able to work with people who have absolute faith in you to fix everything.

Salary:
Approximately **negative $220,000** per child over 18 years.

Work Environment:
Others in this job commonly describe working conditions as "isolating." Some report that through a combination of their own efforts and happenstance they have been able to build a support system. This is to be done on your own time, without guidance.

Status:
Varies. While it is often called the most important job in the world, in practice, it will often feel like the least appreciated job in the world. Validation tends to be private and internal, while rewards often come in small packages (cute and utterly adorable small packages).

Rewards:
Immeasurable and unbeatable.

We know that parenting is far too absorbing and multifaceted to be reduced to a job listing, but we hope that this little exercise makes it clear that as fun, rewarding, and meaningful as parenting is, it is also labor-intensive, challenging, and non-stop. And, it is made even harder when expectations, preparations, and messages from others are out of step with actual day-to-day experience.

So on the day the crying won't stop or the spaghetti ends up on the cat or the *No!-No!-No!s* seem never-ending, it is easy to see how mom begins to wonder what she is doing wrong or why she isn't as happy as she is supposed to be. And please let this not be the same day that a well-meaning but naïve stranger looks at her and her beautiful child and exclaims, *"Aren't you having so much fun?!"*

GROWTH: IT'S NOT JUST FOR KIDS

Alongside the everyday demands of caretaking young children, there is another kind of hard work that parents do. This work, which we *also* don't tend to talk about much, is the *emotional work* of coming to know oneself as a mom or a dad.

Parenthood can broaden and even shift one's own identity. Many new parents report that they are suddenly reflecting more (and sometimes from a renewed perspective) on their own upbringing, their values, and their goals. This personal journey can be unexpected, unnerving, enriching, rewarding; in truth, it can be anything, including resisted. But no matter how we respond to this nudge towards self-exploration, our response is part of the emotional work of being a parent.

In the toddler years, this emotional work can intensify. The nudge, in fact, can begin to feel a lot more like a push. As our infants grow into walking and exploring children who are able to throw, hit, and scream, we can suddenly find ourselves thrust into new (and not always welcome) roles—one day mom might feel like a warden, another day like a punching bag.

For many, **figuring out how to respond to behaviors we want to discourage is one of greatest challenges of parenting.** It asks us to do the emotional work of discovering and deciding (and rediscovering and re-deciding) how we balance the *soft side of love* and the *firm side of love*. This work can be more challenging when there is cultural confusion around the concepts of love and discipline, specifically the oft-made assumption that love feels comfortable and conflict-free, while discipline equals punishment and fighting. Quite the opposite, we are often at our most loving when we are being a parental leader.

Whether we use the terms *soft side/firm side of love*, *love/discipline*, or *warmth/control*, these essential components of parenting are *both* expressions of love, and *both* are necessary for the physical and emotional well being of children. At each encounter with our child we pull from the warmth and control sides of love—choosing, balancing, and adjusting as we decide, for instance, *"Is this behavior related to being tired or ill?" "Does my child need to know that the choice will have consequences?" "Does my child need more time and support to develop the skill?"*

Figuring out the answer that works best for the absolutely unique you, your absolutely unique child, and your absolutely unique relationship at this absolutely unique moment in time is why **parenting is an art—always practiced by you, the parent, but supported by others.**

We are grateful you have chosen this book to be part of your support network. Over the next few pages you will find one arm of that support in the form of brief exercises related to temperament and parenting style. Not only are they helpful for exploring and understanding our children and ourselves, they point the way to specific strategies and practical approaches that can help ease or avoid the eruptions and disruptions of the day.

TEMPERAMENT

The mother-child bond, in particular, has been held up to such an idealized and exalted image, that there can be a false assumption that a mother should automatically and instantaneously know her child.

The reality is, as with any relationship, mom and child *grow* to know one another, as do dad and child. The relationship, though, is not like any other; parent and child are uniquely intertwined both emotionally and physically, and as caretakers, mom and dad are highly motivated to be attuned to the child quickly and thoroughly.

Temperament—your's and your child's—plays an important role in the parent-child relationship, and understanding temperament—*your's and your child's*—can help you to more easily understand and respond to your child's cues and feelings, as well as your own.

Differences, or even similarities, in temperament may help explain some of those days that just do not go well.

An out-going dad may be surprised at what overwhelms or upsets a child with a more introverted disposition. A "low-sensitivity" mom might become impatient with a "high-sensitivity" child who is bothered by the itchy tag on his shirt and can't do anything else until it is fixed.

At the same time, **similar temperaments come with their own challenges.** For instance, parents might not

---

Nine Traits of Temperament

A person will have varying levels and combinations of these traits.

- Activity
- Adaptability
- Rhythmicity or Regularity
- Sensitivity
- Distractibility
- Persistence
- Intensity
- Mood
- High Approach/More cautious

(Source: Dr. S. Chess & Dr. A. Thomas)

always find it easy to help their children through situations that they themselves still find challenging. Likewise, a parent who has struggled with a personality trait—a dad who, for example, connects his tendency towards distractibility to his past difficulties in school—can overreact or become impatient or worried when he sees the same trait in his child.

As these examples show, it's important to understand your own temperament, your child's, as well as the temperaments of those central to your family life. It's also important to know in your heart that no temperament is superior or inferior.

SUPPORTING YOUR OWN TEMPERAMENT
Becoming aware of temperament will help you help your child, but don't forget to use it to help yourself, too.

- **Are you more cautious in temperament?** Then arrive at the playdate early so that you can enter into a smaller more manageable group; or make it a point to organize one-on-one-playdates.

- **Do you need more social stimulation than your child?** Then absolutely make sure you set up adult time to be with your own friends and be as social and gregarious as you want to be. This is not an indulgence. It is necessary for you.

- **Are you highly active?** Then you will need to arrange with family or friends for "run time" if you've been trapped indoors for days with a child who has been ill.

Remember, our children learn most from what we do. If you want your child to grow up to value herself and her own needs, you need to value yours too. **Becoming a mom (or becoming a dad) never means you stop being you.**

What You Need to Know About Temperament

- We are, as current thinking holds, born with it.

- No temperament is better than any other. Each has its strengths and challenges.

- Temperament is resistant to change, but while a more introverted person may never become an extrovert, she can learn to comfortably do, and excel at, "extroverted" things such as lead and speak to large groups.

- Temperament is different from age-appropriate behaviors. Most toddlers need to be active; this does not necessarily mean they have a high-activity temperament.

- Parents, family dynamics, and environment can influence how a child expresses his temperament.

- Temperament traits are not either-or; each trait lies along a spectrum.

TEMPERAMENT TOOL

This exercise is not the only way to understand temperament, nor is it meant to peg people into certain categories. It is a tool that may aid your exploration towards a better understanding of yourself, those you love, and the relationships between you and your loved ones.

In each box, mark the point along the continuum that best represents your child's expression of that particular trait. Do the same for yourself. **As you do this exercise, don't think too hard: Trust your gut**. You very likely already have a strong intuitive understanding. For instance, before the child speaks her first word, a mom may hear herself reassuring well-intentioned relatives that her child enjoys a slower pace when meeting new people. Another parent may have learned that her child is so anxious to engage with a new activity she can hardly get the coat off fast enough.

As you do this exercise, also **consider age and development.** For example: Toddlers are active little people. How much your child exhausts you is probably not the best measure of his activity level, consider instead his level of activity compared to his peers. Keep in mind, too, that **each point along the continuum represents a normal range of behavior.** This means that whether high or low reactive, whether predictable or unpredictable, no expression of any trait is more "normal" than another.

Once you have completed each box for your child and then for yourself, you will have a good picture of your child's temperament and your own. Importantly, you also have an easy-to-read visual representation of the ways in which you and your child are similar in temperament and the ways in which you are different.

ACTIVITY LEVEL

	High Activity		Low Activity	
MY CHILD	· · · · ·	· · · · ·
ME	· · · · ·	· · · · ·
_____	· · · · ·	· · · · ·

REGULARITY

	Predictable		Unpredicatable	
MY CHILD	· · · · ·	· · · · ·
ME	· · · · ·	· · · · ·
_____	· · · · ·	· · · · ·

APPROACH/WITHDRAWAL

	Joins Easily		Observes Before Joining	
MY CHILD	· · · · ·	· · · · ·
ME	· · · · ·	· · · · ·
_____	· · · · ·	· · · · ·

ADAPTABILITY

	Accepts Change Easily	Resists Change
MY CHILD	· · · · ·	· · · · ·
ME	· · · · ·	· · · · ·
_____	· · · · ·	· · · · ·

SENSITIVITY

	High Reaction	Low Reaction
MY CHILD	· · · · ·	· · · · ·
ME	· · · · ·	· · · · ·
_____	· · · · ·	· · · · ·

MOOD

	Pleasant	Negative
MY CHILD	· · · · ·	· · · · ·
ME	· · · · ·	· · · · ·
_____	· · · · ·	· · · · ·

PERSISTENCE

	Persistent	Changeable
MY CHILD	· · · · ·	· · · · ·
ME	· · · · ·	· · · · ·
_____	· · · · ·	· · · · ·

DISTRACTIBILITY

	High	Low
MY CHILD	· · · · ·	· · · · ·
ME	· · · · ·	· · · · ·
_____	· · · · ·	· · · · ·

INTENSITY

	Strong	Subdued
MY CHILD	· · · · ·	· · · · ·
ME	· · · · ·	· · · · ·
_____	· · · · ·	· · · · ·

Next, ask yourself who else is important to your family or to your child. It might be a spouse or co-parent, a sibling, grandparent, nanny, or other caregiver. You'll see there is a third line in each box. We encourage you to use this (and to add as many lines as needed) to understand the temperament and interactions of temperament of others central to your family life.

Finally, now that you have a better understanding of the temperaments in your family, let's look briefly at what all this means in the ebb and flow of a day with a toddler.

TEMPERAMENT & PARENTING

When you understand temperament you are more equipped to guide and support your child. For instance:

- When you know you have a high activity child, you know that planning for a long car ride means also planning for stops along the way, and, perhaps, being ready with some movement songs for the car seat or to smooth the way back into the car seat.

- When you know your child is easily distracted, you may find redirecting from the dog's water bowl an inconvenience, but not particularly challenging. On the other hand, a highly persistent child would more likely benefit from a gate (or some other management of the environment) until she learns to respect the dog's need for water.

Understanding temperament can diffuse blame and judgment, and help you to *know* and *accept* your child as the whole, unique person that he is.

A low-active mom with a high active child might worry that her child is wild, out-of-control. "He is driving me crazy," she might say (*and feel*). Driven by her own need for calm, she may respond by trying to forcibly contain his energy. Because **we have a strong tendency to see *our* norm as *the* norm**, mom may believe that there is something wrong with her child.

When mom understands temperament, she can make environmental adjustments so that his expression of his temperament is better supported, and though mom will very likely still be challenged by the differences in temperament, the challenge is now emptied of labels and the language of blame or assumed intent to drive someone crazy.

Of course, mom will still worry about her child. If not now, there will be something later. Parents worry. And that worry should be acknowledged for the resource that it is. But it is a much better resource, a more useful and effective resource and, for the parent, a much healthier resource, when it has an informed base of knowledge to check in with. Temperament is an important piece of this knowledge base, as are child development and age-appropriateness (fortunately, this book is full of information about both).

PARENTING STYLE

As mentioned already, loving our children can nudge us to reflect on how we were loved as children. This reflection, when we take it on, can become a powerful source for understanding who we are as parents, as well as who we want to be and how we might get there.

The *Parenting Styles Chart* on the next page assists this process of reflection. The information in the chart is based on decades of research and is a standard model in the field of psychology for understanding parental behaviors and resulting outcomes in child behavior.

But, and we cannot emphasize this enough, the model offers *broad* categories that describe *underlying patterns* of parenting behavior. This means that though the chart is made up of four quadrants, representing four categories, there are in fact a myriad

of possible points within each quadrant. The graph attempts to visually sort the ways in which the elements of parenting—warmth and control—are maintained in balance or are distorted by a perceived lack of one or the other or both.

As you consider each category, it should be with the understanding that a short-term and close-up view may have you jumping between quadrants. What you are looking for is the overall pattern of behavior you experienced as a child, and that you offer now as a parent.

There is considerable research on the effects each parenting style can have on children. These outcomes are, of course, influenced by other factors, one of which is temperament. As an example: research shows that children who have experienced autocratic/rigid parenting are at a greater risk of being withdrawn and overly compliant, *and* they are also at a greater risk of rebellious and defiant behavior. These opposite outcomes are reflective of innate differences in temperament that would have one child turn inward and the other more outward.

Parenting styles and child outcomes is itself a book-length topic, but when it comes to the toddler, what's most important to understand about parental styles and resulting outcomes for children is the effect on attachment.

PARENTING STYLES & ATTACHMENT

Attachment is everything to the very young. Without it, the toddler does not thrive. With it, her whole world works. From positive attachment grows positive discipline, positive empathy, and long-term positive relationships. Parenting style is key to the development and maintenance of attachment ... or lack thereof.

Rigid/Autocratic

POSSIBLE BELIEF SYSTEM:

I'm the parent, I decide.

WHAT IT CAN LOOK LIKE AT THIS AGE:

- Harsh tones
- Hand slaps
- Threats
  If you don't, I won't.. Stop it!

PARENT CAN BE:

- Dismissive of child's feelings
- Unaccommodating of developmental stage

Authoritative/Democratic

POSSIBLE BELIEF SYSTEM:

Everyone in this family counts. My job is to love, coach, and guide.

WHAT IT CAN LOOK LIKE AT THIS AGE:

- Free cuddles & smiles
- Rhythm to the day
- Acknowledgement rather than praise:
  I see you climbing the slide ladder, are you proud?
- Collaborating with the child to problem solve (not abdicating to the child)

PARENT CAN BE:

- Firm, but not rigid
- Respectful
- Cooperative
- Loving

MORE CONTROL

LESS WARMTH   *MORE WARMTH*

Uninvolved/Distracted

POSSIBLE BELIEF SYSTEM:

Kids don't count as much as adults
OR
Kids are often in the way.

WHAT IT CAN LOOK LIKE AT THIS AGE:

- Child is passed to anyone
- Lack of physical/ emotional order to the day
- Eat when it's convenient for mom/dad
- Childcare is inconsistent, sometimes not safe

PARENT CAN:

- Relinquish decision-making
- Relinquish discipline to other adults

Indulgent/Lax

POSSIBLE BELIEF SYSTEM:

I'm a good parent when my child is happy.

WHAT IT CAN LOOK LIKE AT THIS AGE:

- Play room with toys everywhere!
- Good job! (Praise for everything)
- Overwhelming attention
- Few rules imposed on the child. [Potential parent martyr]

PARENT CAN:

- Be affectionate
- Have difficulty saying *No*
- Use bribery

LESS CONTROL

Rigid parenting of infants and toddlers places them at risk of tentative attachment to their caregivers. If adults respond in ways that the child experiences as harsh, unpredictable, or frightening it is much more difficult for the child to be secure in their belief that they are loved, as well as to trust that the world is a safe place to explore.

Uninvolved parenting of infants and toddlers places them at risk of becoming unattached, perhaps unable to develop the ability to attach to another. In this case, it may not be the adult who is experienced as harsh, unpredictable or frightening, but the whole of life! Because these children still have the internal developmental drive to explore, their explorations may result in injury to body and mind, as well as spirit.

Indulgent parenting of infants and toddlers places them at risk through "too much of a good thing." Having an engaged parent is good, but when life/play (play being the work of the exploring toddler) is too often parent-led, it can limit the child too much. It can interfere with the child's personal initiative and later ability to self-regulate. Attachment and intrusiveness may then become fused.

Authoritative parenting of infants and toddlers creates the context in which secure attachment can most often occur. Authoritative parents are trustworthy both in their expressions of love and care, but also in managing the environment in which children can explore to their fullest while being safe. Those regular naps and meal times are not just for physical well-being, when implemented with the warmth of an Authoritative parent they create an emotional climate in which to thrive.

As we shared already in the Introduction, all of the advice and information that you will encounter in this book is centered within that upper right quadrant labeled Authoritative/Democratic.

The parenting styles chart is a useful tool for thinking about the parenting that you received, and perhaps to better understand others in your life. For some, knowing the power of a parenting style can be reassuring in the face of expectations of friends and extended family whose patterns you can now understand more fully. But, because of what we know and what we see and experience from a parenting research and education base, when it comes to the nurturing of children, Authoritative/Democratic is the corner we hope parents will live in most of the time.

Many "parenting style" discussions and charts published in books and online focus on behaviors and outcomes that pertain to older children. We have framed this discussion to be relevant to you *now* as you are creating the context for your on-going parent leadership style.

PART 2: GLANCE & GO GUIDES

Meltdowns

Why not call it a Tantrum? *Meltdown* describes a physiological process. *Tantrum* implies an intentionality that is not appropriate at this age.

TIRED

ITCHY FEET, ITCHY FEET, ITCHY FEET!

EMPTY TUMMY

Meltdowns are perfectly normal. This in no way makes them easy to watch. Because they often have a physical root—hunger, tiredness, overstimulation or some other discomfort—attention to these kinds of stressors can help stave off meltdowns. But despite your care and diligence, meltdowns may still happen. The important fact to know is that *at this age* a meltdown is a biological response; it is not a willful action. This means neither you nor your child can order it to stop. Instead, the toddler needs to do the hard work of regaining control over his body, and he needs you to help.

The Role of Physiology

The toddler's central nervous system can become overwhelmed and crash—just like a computer. Hunger, tiredness, too much stimuli, discomfort, and frustration are common loads that build until the body crashes. Often, the back will arch, the limbs will flail, and the body will literally flop to the floor. These are all signs of a normal, but young and still developing, central nervous system attempting to release energy that, for the moment, it cannot process or control.

The toddler is not a small adult.

The child's body cannot manage lack of food, lack of sleep or a hurried schedule as well as an adult body (which does not necessarily manage these stressors all that easily). The toddler has not yet developed the internal resources that adults use every day. For instance, imagine an adult and a child standing in line. Both are bored and impatient. The adult understands time. She can remind herself why she is standing in line, or calm herself with the thought that later she will go on a run. The toddler lives in the moment. He is without the simple coping strategies that adults often take for granted.

Meltdowns:
Use these steps to help your toddler regain control of his or her body

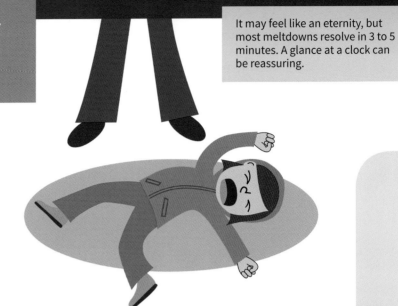

It may feel like an eternity, but most meltdowns resolve in 3 to 5 minutes. A glance at a clock can be reassuring.

FIRST
Ensure the SAFETY of the child, yourself and others.

Be CALM—in body, in language, in facial expression, in attitude.

ALSO Reduce STIMULI.

QUIET THE ENVIRONMENT
Turn off TV, radio, and dim bright lights.

OFF!

QUIET YOURSELF
YOU are typically the most stimulating element of a child's environment. This is not the time to overload a child with directives—*calm down, calm down*—or questions—*what's wrong, honey?*— or discipline—*if you don't stop, I'll…* If safety is ensured, (watchfully) ignore the meltdown.

IF safety is an issue and/or the meltdown does not resolve itself in 3 to 5 minutes try any or all of the following tools [🔧]:

You are not failing as a parent when your child is expressing her full range of humanity.

Protect yourself: Keep his head below your chin.

Arms are NOT held to his sides but brought to his chest. This is more comforting.

COCOON From behind, hold your body against his. Bring his arms in to hug his chest. His head is against your sternum (which can take a hard bang better than the chin). The hold is firm—not with angry strait-jacket muscles, but the muscles of someone offering love and care. This cocoon hold helps the young body CENTER itself.

ROCK Calmly and rhythmically rock the child. If he has not yet regained physical control use the COCOON hold while rocking.

DRINK OF WATER
Calmly offer the child a GLASS OF WATER. Because swallowing demands rhythm and control, this can be an extremely effective method for returning a child's system to a regulated state.

RHYTHM SOUNDS Sooth the child with gentle rhythmic humming or swishing sounds—*ums, ahs and uh-huhs*— that are soft and comforting.

WHEN you must move the child:

SAFE CARRY
Pick him up from behind. Because an arching back is a normal physiological response of a stressed central nervous system, his body should face forward so that he cannot arch out of your arms (also, so that he cannot bite).

Hold him against your midsection and hips so that kicking or flailing legs cannot harm you. For the same reason, hold his arms against his body. Active support communicates: *I will help you but I will not let you hurt me.*

WHEN it's over:

IT'S OVER
Do not belabor or punish. It's time for a fresh start.

You are helping your child but you are not letting your child hurt you.

Look at little Jimmy—he's practicing control of his central nervous system again!

Is my child having too many meltdowns?

There is no magic formula that answers this question. Meltdowns are normal, but a child who has multiple meltdowns and can't consistently self-calm in 3–5 minutes may need additional support.

If you are concerned, track the FREQUENCY, INTENSITY, and DURATION (noting the time of day).

The solution may be as simple as tweaking the family schedule. But if adjustments have no effect, the child may benefit from a pediatric physical/occupational therapy assessment. Remember, the purpose is not to label the child, but to find tools to help him. A therapist may be able to offer play-based techniques that will enhance the child's ability to manage the physical demands of the day.

Why can't I just give her what she wants?

Because she may just learn that using her body intensely and destructively is a very effective way to get you to do what she wants.

What if it happens in a public place?

The same strategies apply. Remember your child is your priority. Try to: (1) pretend no one else is there; (2) tell yourself that all eyes on you are sympathetic and supportive (surely, many are); and (3) If someone offers help, and your good judgment concurs, take it (though your child remains 100% in your care). Sometimes the surprise attention of a friendly stranger can help a child to center herself.

Yes, it is normal. Meltdowns are:

- one way a child practices self-control.
- a sign of independence and a burgeoning awareness that the world does not center only on the self.
- nonetheless, stressful.

Is it really not willful?

The toddler is testing the waters of a very big world. True explorations of power come later. No matter how it originated, one meltdown is the same as any other. The child must do the same hard work to regain control.

Caregiver Reminders:

- It can be difficult to be in the face of big emotions, especially those—such as anger—that we have been taught to contain or avoid. Remember, children have not yet learned to moderate intensity of expression.

- Although your toddler is becoming more and more verbal every day, the tools we use with a newborn are never lost. Facial expression and pitches in tone are always key communicators.

- Today's meltdown is not a sign of who your child will be at age 14.

Transitions

Every day is filled with transitions: wake up, clothes on, mealtime, shoes on, in the car, out of the car, playground!, naptime, diaper change, big sister home, dinner, stroll, clean-up time, bath, stories, into bed, sleep.

Toddlers live in the moment. Unable to envision the trajectory of the day or to rely on autopilot, the toddler is uniquely challenged by the routine stops and starts of daily life. Preparation—telling the child about the change before it happens and as it happens— can ease the stress of transitions. Tools that signal change and offer focus can help the child shift from one activity to the next, while rituals and routines can provide anchors in a day filled with constant stimuli and little control.

The Role of Physiology

The toddler brain has not yet developed EXECUTIVE FUNCTION—the complex set of mental processes that enables us to plan and organize, to anticipate and adapt, to focus and order, and to understand time and its passing. Imagine one day without Executive Function. You don't know to put shoes on before going out, how long it takes to drive to work, or when a loved one will return. Even oft-repeated tasks—eating, putting on socks—demand your complete attention, while at the same time you are trying to make sense of your body and your environment. This is what every day is like for the toddler. Because his brain is still developing, he needs you, for now, to be his Executive Function and to help buffer the bumps of his day.

A toddler's developmental drive is to be a doer (particularly so for the young toddler). She experiences the world with her whole body. She must run, taste, and climb. Tasks that require stillness—the carseat, the dinner table, sleep—are biologically hard. She may need encouragement, support, empathy, and help to accomplish tasks that are off-step with her internal drive.

Transitions:

Use these steps to help your toddler make the transition from one activity to the next

THE STORY OF GETTING OUT THE DOOR:

Chapter 1
We will eat our cereal.
We will put on our shoes.
We will put on our coat.
We will get in the car and
We will go to the store.

Chapter 2
Cereal all done.
Now we put on shoes.
This one first or the other one first?

Chapter 3
Shoes on! Yay! Now we find our coats. Can you find your coat?
I will find my coat, too.

Chapter 4
We are ready to get in the car and go to the store, where you can sit in the cart and help daddy shop...

FIRST

TELL THE STORY of what will come next.

Give the child a sense of control by offering two acceptable choices.

Allow TIME for the child to take each step.

Model the task for the child by working in parallel.

UPDATE the story as steps are accomplished.

IF

the toddler is UPSET or RESISTING a transition, show empathy.

You wish we could stay. You are sad!

SHOW EMPATHY & GIVE WORDS TO FEELINGS

Give words to the emotion the child is experiencing. Mirror the emotion in your facial expression and body language. The child needs to know you understand that she is upset. Until she does, she is likely to continue to "tell" you.

THEN to support and ease the transition use any or all of these additional transition tools [🔧]:

A child has enough fears. Do not add to them by threatening to leave the child behind.

When we visit the zoo again we will see the gorillas and the lion... maybe the lion will ROAR!...and we will...

At home you can play with your toy lion and tell dad about the zoo. What will you tell him about first?

T USE IMAGINATION
Offer the child in imagination what he cannot have at that moment. Be specific. It may help to add a silly or unexpected element—*Maybe the lion will be having a tea party...*

T LOOK FORWARD
Show the child the future. Be positive about what is next.

T MAKE IT A GAME
Skip. Tip-toe. Walk like an animal. Race. Games make hard work fun and can also become helpful rituals.

T SING A SONG
Specific songs for specific tasks are not only fun, but provide cues to the steps needed to accomplish the task.

You pick up the blue blocks, I'll pick up the red ones

Let's sing our clean-up song:
*We have had a busy day
Time to put our toys away
When we get the job all done
We'll sing and read and have more fun.*

T OBJECT
Bring one along. If it is safe and legal, take one (such as a leaf from the playground). Objects can offer security.

BRRRING!

"Aww! The timer says it's time to go."

T TIMER/CLOCK
Let a timer announce when to leave or to stop. Be your child's partner—you are as disappointed as she is.

"Remember, when you get in your car seat that's when you have your special snack!"

T ACKNOWLEDGEMENT
A special snack, a special book or activity acknowledges the hard work the child is doing.

Remember: Transitions are hard but they do get easier as they are practiced.

What if nothing's working?

With a strong, steady body, calm muscles and firm follow-through, you will have to step in, explaining matter-of-factly as you go: *Can you put your arm in the sleeve or do you need my help? Now I will help you and another day you will be ready to do this.* The child, in all likelihood will be upset. Continue to use Empathy and Naming Feelings and, if you see fit, try some transition tools again.

Is she just defying me?

No. The body language of resistance can look the same in a toddler as in an older child, but the toddler is not engaging in a *willful* power struggle. She is yelling and kicking because she does not want to stop playing with playdoh, but she is not consciously attempting to manipulate. Rather, she has not yet gained control of her emotions and the energy they create within her body.

Isn't what you call "acknowledgement" just a bribe?

Rewards are part of life even for adults. We all find ways to help ourselves complete tasks that are particularly difficult. You can sidestep the language of bribery by avoiding *if-then* statements in favor of *when-then* statements. You are not dangling a reward; you are simply reporting how the world works: *Remember, when you're in your jammies that's when you can pick out two stories!*

Is my child's need for a transitional object a sign of weakness?

No.

Are transition tools just distractions?

Sure, but as with almost every interaction with your child, these tools are always doing more. Songs encourage language development; Empathy and Naming Feelings help develop emotional intelligence; Rituals plant the seeds of autopilot; etc.

You call it walking like a duck. I call it planting the seeds of high-level Executive Function!

Caregiver Reminders:

- A child under 3 is working hard every day to figure out the maze of life. He is trying to make sense of speech, toileting, mealtime, his body—how exactly do these legs work?—and his relationships—who do I belong to? We don't always see the hard work of the toddler because, to us, it looks like play.

- Transitions are not only changes the child engages in, but changes to the child's environment, such as the reentry of a parent who has been working outside the home or a sibling who has been at school.

SETTING THE GROUNDWORK FOR SMOOTHER TRANSITIONS

1 Ask yourself if your expectations are realistic. Is the day too hurried? Is the child asked to get in the car seat too often or expected to sit still too long? See if you can adjust your expectations, while keeping your values intact. For instance, if you value family mealtime but you have a child who prefers to graze on small meals throughout the day, one compromise is to allow a toy or crayon to occupy the child at the table, or to permit the child who has finished eating to play at your feet.

2 Create rituals around things that you do everyday. Start with those that occur around the same time each day. Examples include a tiny-people chore before mealtime (carry spoons to the table) or a nightly piggy-back ride to bed. Rituals and routines can provide anchors in a chaotic world.

3 Create opportunities for the child to experience control and competency. For instance: offer two choices, both of which you can live with *(Frog boots today or blue shoes? Jammies first or brush teeth?)*; demonstrate the task by working in parallel *(Mama's putting her shoe on, too. We're both picking up toys!)*; act inept to let the child show-off his abilities *(Gloves go on feet, right? I can't find the gate to leave the playground? I wonder who can show me...).*

4 Make it visual. Have a calendar or chart with pictures representing what will happen that day. When transitioning to bedtime, for instance, the child can mark off each before-bed task as it is accomplished.

5 When possible be flexible. If the child is MEGA-resistant, let natural consequences communicate the rule: *The playspace teacher says we have to wear shoes. We can go play when you get your shoes on. We can watch until you're ready.*

Playing Well with Others: Hitting, Shoving, Biting

Though hitting, shoving and biting are typically called "aggressive behaviors," we do not use this label because it implies an intention *to hurt* that is not appropriate at the toddler age.

A toddler may hit out of frustration or simply to say "Hi. I am here." A toddler may bite out of anger, or to relieve the twinge of new teeth. A child may shove because it is the quickest way to get to a toy, or because he is tired and overloaded. While the underlying reason for the child's behavior will influence how you respond, it is absolutely vital that you respond immediately and effectively. To help your toddler, you must ensure that: these behaviors are never rewarded; they do not get the child excess attention; they do not get the child what he wants. Also, your toddler needs you to show him acceptable methods of expression, and he needs you to help him channel his physical energy in a safe way.

The Role of Physiology.

A young child cannot anticipate injury either to herself or to others. She is still developing the cause-and-effect thinking that allows her to connect the hit to the hurt. Likewise, the toddler does not fully grasp the boundaries between self and others. Thus, she cannot yet use her own experience (*That hurts me*) to understand or predict the experience of others (*It must hurt him too*).

Self-control and delayed gratification (commonly called IMPULSE CONTROL) are not easy skills to learn, nor to practice. Credit card debt and diet books remind us that impulse control is hard even for adults. Yet, toddlers must practice impulse control without the developmental tools adults rely on. The frontal lobes—where the brain does the work of impulse control—are not fully developed in the toddler. Nor has the toddler mastered the powerful coping tools available to us through verbal communication, and he does not necessarily have the physical coordination to stop a pat-pat-pat from becoming a whomp-whomp-whomp. It is *biologically* difficult for the toddler to control his body and his emotions. In order to play safely with others, he will need our help and guidance.

Playing Well With Others:

What to do when your child hits, shoves, kicks, or bites

FIRST

Respond IMMEDIATELY
Make it SAFE
TEND to the other child FIRST, physically and emotionally

YOUR ATTENTION...
not only reassures the OTHER child, it teaches YOUR child that hurting others does not get *him* attention.

> George was so excited to see you. He didn't remember to use his words to say Hi.

> That was a big surprise when George knocked you down.

Have your child overhear the lesson.

ALSO

> Hitting hurts.

Do NOT let your child BENEFIT
If she has pushed to get to the slide, take her off it. If he has hit to get a toy, do not allow him to use it. Avoid wrestling the toy away. Immobilize it. What is important is that the child is unable to use it.

SHOW that the behavior is UNACCEPTABLE
Your facial expression and tone of voice send a clear message. A lecture does not.

THE BITE: Because a bite can be biologically based, it may help to offer a chew toy or wet washcloth to relieve the tension of new teeth. But always do this ALONG WITH the behavioral training, so that the accidental bite does not turn into a functional tool.

THEN use any or all of the following tools [🔧] as best fits you, your child, and the situation, taking into account the motivation and the intensity of the act.

Because lecturing is a lot of "face-time" it may unintentionally reinforce the behavior.

CONNECT THE ACT TO ITS EFFECT
(Best for older or early verbal toddler)
Help your child see the results of his action by describing the visual and audio cues from the other child. You are reporting, not blaming.

> See Lola's face. Hear her crying. That push and fall was a big hurt.

> Tearful eyes and crying sounds are some of the ABCs of social language that your child is learning.

MODEL HOW TO USE THE BODY
(Best if child has hurt or overwhelmed another as a greeting or to get their attention)
Teach your child and model for her how we greet people and how we get someone's attention. Draw a picture in her mind with descriptive words and body language:

> When we see Charlie we look at his face and we say "Hi Charlie."

> You can bring Nadia a toy to show her you want to play together.

OFFER AN OPPORTUNITY TO HELP (TO ATONE)
Show and/or narrate how to make it better. Do not force help on a child who does not want it; nor on a child who cannot, at that moment, give it. Whether it is a day when your child actively helps, watches you help, or simply hears your description of how to help, all will plant the seeds of compassion.

> Maybe a drink of water will help Lola. Let's go together to get a drink for your friend.

OR

> Lola's tears are saying that she was not done with that toy yet. It is time to give it back. Can you do it, or will Mama help you?

TEACH TOUCH
(Especially helpful for learning to be safe with pets and babies)
Give concrete meaning to the abstract word. For example, repeat the word "gentle" as you physically guide the child's hand in a gentle touch. In this way she can feel, understand, and practice giving a gentle touch.

REMOVE THE CHILD
(Best for very young toddler, a bite, or a particularly angry or resistant act)

BRIEFLY SEPARATE:
Separate the child from play and from your attention for one and a half to two minutes. After: do not lecture or demand remorse. Simply ask: *Ready to play again?* (Reflection comes in later years)

END PLAY/GO HOME:
If it happens again or your gut tells you it might, your child is showing you that now is not a good time to play with others. Report the reason for leaving: *It is too hard for you to play safe today. We will try again another day.*

AFTER a hit, bite, or shove you must be extra vigilant to prevent another.
For the safety of others and to teach and support your child, stay physically near (*shadow*) your child as he plays. See pages 44 and 71 for a detailed description of shadowing.

Showing a child how to be successful is more helpful than retelling her failures.

Playing Well With YOU:

What to do when your child hits, kicks, or bites you

While it is natural for children to test most those they trust most, you are not your child's punching bag.

STOP! #*%&@...

FIRST
Respond IMMEDIATELY
Ignoring teaches that the behavior is acceptable. Responding big only after you have hit your limit teaches that the behavior gets LOTS of attention.

Wow! that gets her attention!

NOT RESPONDING   NOT RESPONDING   NOT RESPONDING   RESPONDING TOO LATE

ALSO
Show that the behavior is UNSAFE, UNACCEPTABLE, and UNREWARDING:
The tone and tenor of your response will depend on the motivation behind the behavior, as well as your child's physical and emotional state.

OW! That hit hurt daddy!

Don't give in (though you can offer support)

I know you want to play, but your hit hurt me and I can't play right now. I wonder if Teddy wants to keep you company while you wait.

Your face makes it clear that this is serious and that it is not a game.

Let her see the result of her action.

YOU MAY ALSO WANT TO:
- Offer or accept your child's participation in your care.
- Time-out for 1–2 minutes. (again, depending on intensity and intention)
- Alter plans. The behavior may be a sign that his reserves are low. Always explain so that the child knows it was not the hit that was successful.

THEN use any or all of the following tools [🔧] as best fits you, your child, and the situation, taking into account the motivation and the intensity of the act.

In the eyes of a child a hit or bite that is IGNORED is a hit or bite that is ACCEPTABLE.

T **IF YOUR CHILD DOES NOT CALM**
When the child is being continually and repeatedly aggressive with you, immobilize her arms (or legs) firmly, but gently as you address her frustration. The firm hold communicates the social rule that hurting is not allowed.

Another option, if circumstances allow, is to redirect the intensity in a safe way, such as by suggesting she sing at the top of her lungs.

> If it escalates into a meltdown, you are now responding to a meltdown (p. 31) not a hit, kick, or bite.

T **IF IT WAS ACCIDENTAL (AN EXPRESSION OF ENERGY OR EXPERIMENTATION)**
State the social rule (*People are hurt when toys are thrown, keep your trucks on the floor*) and provide a safe alternative for the child to explore his physical abilities and express his physical energy (*Let's see if you can throw these soft toys into the basket.*)

T **IF IT WAS TO INTERRUPT YOU**
Remind and model appropriate ways to get your attention. As you describe the desired behavior, also demonstrate it.

> Did you want to say hi to me? Remember you can come in front of me so I can see your face and you can put your hand on my arm.

WHEN he does it right:

When your child does ask for your attention in an appropriate way, you must respond. This does not mean doing what he wants (that is a separate issue). It does mean:

- Acknowledging his accomplishment,
- Replying, and
- Supporting him through the answer.

Give him a big smile:
> You knew how to get my attention!

Reply to his request:
> I can play with you after I'm done talking to Julie's mom.

Support the wait:
> Come here and hold my hand while you wait.

OR

> Go pick out two cars for us to play with.

FOLLOW THROUGH
Don't make him wait long.
[If you need to, set a timer for 2 minutes so that the wait is not too long and you are held to your promise.]

Because we are social creatures negative attention is better than none.

Should I make my child apologize?

Demanding that a toddler say "sorry" risks teaching that there is a magic word that gets her off the hook. Your immediate response and attention to the victim will build an understanding of the meaning behind "sorry"—*I behaved in a way that broke trust and caused harm, I understand I need to change that behavior*. Also, for the child who has been hurt, more meaningful than an *abstract* "sorry" is the *concrete* attention and help of adults, whose actions reassure that what happened will not be allowed to happen again.

Isn't this a phase he will grow out of?

As he grows your child will gain better control of his body and he will rely more on his verbal skills as they become as powerful as his motor skills. BUT, if hitting or biting has been ignored and/or has benefited the child, it will become a learned, reinforced, and on-going behavior.

Does wrestling with my child encourage these behaviors?

Modeling how to be strong and not to cause harm is a wonderful gift to give to your child. Wrestling and active play also provide opportunities to practice body control and to teach the difference between touch that is soft, medium, and hard. Be sure to set clear boundaries of *when*, *where*, and *with whom* we wrestle.

Caregiver Reminders:

- It is common to develop an awareness that something is not allowed and still not be able to stop oneself from doing it. The glimmer of understanding is an important step along your child's learning curve.

- Don't burden your child with a label. No toddler is a Biter or a Hitter. Rather, if your child is biting or hitting he is showing you he is not yet able to play safely without adult support.

- Your toddler needs your guidance and attention as she learns to be with others. But you need social time, too. Don't depend on your child's playdate for your social needs. Enjoy grown-up "playdates" with your grown-up friends.

- Your small child cannot be expected to read the social cues that guide our interactions with others. He will need your help (*Looks like that hug is too big for Sam. He needs a softer hug*).

SETTING THE GROUNDWORK FOR PLAYING WELL WITH OTHERS...

1 Shadow the young child at play. This means being physically near in order to: maintain safety; redirect energy (*Looks like you want to use muscles too big for your friend. You can use your big muscles over here*); and respond so that a behavior does not go unnoticed and thus, inadvertently, become reinforced. See page 71 of the Playdate Guide for more on shadowing.

2 Prepare your child (*We are going to Ann's house. Do you remember how to say hi when we see Ann?*). Describe what the child WILL do (*You will look for Ann's face and say Hi*), not what he should NOT do (*You won't knock her down from behind like last time*).

3 Create opportunities to practice body control through music and games (such as freeze dance and ring around the rosie); and also through play: *Do you remember how our car stops? Show me how you can make your car stop before it hits the chair.*

4 Use musical play to gauge your child's abilities. If she cannot stop when the music says, "all fall down," it will be even harder to stop when it is not a game and she is under stress. Musical play can help you measure how much shadowing your child will need.

5 When does your child behave best? In smaller groups? Short visits? With certain friends but not others? In environments that you know will be more challenging for your child, you will need to be extra attentive and direct with your help and support.

...AND WITH YOU

Reassurance is a powerful tool. Your child loves your attention. The frustration of not getting it is often the motivation behind hurting you. Here are two tips to help your child feel your attention and still allow you a bit of time and focus directed elsewhere:

1 Throughout the day include some short intervals (10-20 mins.) of absolute undivided attention. Often as the child gets absorbed in the play, your attention can quietly move on.

2 Use small gestures that let your child know you see him and are with him: If he is interrupting, you may increase the chances of being able to finish your conversation by reaching out and laying a hand on his or inviting him to sit in your lap as you talk.

Whining

Whining is irritating, but it is also a survival tool. The challenge is to learn appropriate use. Because whining is an all-ages tool, it's a lesson that will likely need repeating throughout life, even into adulthood.

MOM-EEEE!

Toddlers are dependent on adults for their most basic needs—food, protection, security, comfort. To survive, they must be able to get the attention of adults. Because the grating sound of a whine is so difficult to ignore, it can be an effective way to get that attention. Whining becomes a problem, though, when it is used not as a signal of true distress, but as a normal way to communicate. When your child whines, the first challenge is to discern whether it is signaling a problem that must be tended to. If, instead, the whine is an expression of inconvenience, impatience, or dissatisfaction, the challenge becomes **not** to respond to a request made with a whine. Then, teach and model for your child what kinds of sounds you will respond to (even if your response is still a no).

The Role of Physiology

Why is whining so irritating? Because it is linked to our survival. The grating complaint of a whine shares the same pitches and tones of an infant's distressed cry, as well as the moans and groans of a person in pain. Adult ears are hard-wired to respond to these pitches and tones. Whining is *supposed* to get under our skin. It is part of the built-in feedback loop that ensures our babies are warm and fed, and the hurt are helped. Whining will sometimes be the first clue that your child is sick or somehow distressed.

But, just as a fever can be distressing to a child, so can not getting a cookie when *"I really, really want one!"* Because whining is a sound we unintentionally start to make when we feel bad, it is easy to whine inappropriately—when things don't go our way, when we are inconvenienced or impatient. While we never outgrow the ability to whine, children will naturally rely more on this biologically-based call for help because they are less able to help themselves. Adding to this, toddlers have not yet developed the problem-solving center of the brain and the ability to regulate emotions. Thus, they lack the mental tools needed to resolve frustrations on their own and to moderate their emotions in the face of these frustrations.

Whining:
What to do to stop the whine

NOT SURE?
1. Trust your gut
2. Err on the side of support and help

FIRST Determine the Why of the Whine

IF

the whine is rooted in a real and strong physical distress, such as exhaustion or the first stage of a cold, then:

SUPPORT AND HELP YOUR CHILD

Save the behavioral training for another time.

IF NOT

teach that whining is *not* an acceptable way to communicate:

DO NOT RESPOND TO THE WHINE

- Do not meet a request that is made with a whine.
- Pretend as if you cannot understand words that are spoken in a whine.

THE ART OF IGNORING

Though parents are often advised to *simply* "ignore the whine," ignoring is far from *simple*. To ignore does not mean to be silent, nor should it ever feel like a snub.

- Ignoring is not only about words. When your body stiffens, your shoulders tense, you quicken your pace, or furrow your brow, you are *not* ignoring; you are *responding*.
- Your silence won't help the child be successful. Though to get your message to your child, it's often helpful to direct your words to someone else, the thin air, or even the family pet.

Silliness can be a great cure for a child's frustration, as well as your own. Pulling on your own reserves of humor can help you to teach with a light touch.

THEN show your child how to make a request you CAN respond to. The following tools [🔧] can help.

Remember: Behaviors tend to escalate before they change. Be persistent and patient.

USE WHEN-THEN TO TEACH WHAT SOUNDS ARE SUCCESSFUL

Avoiding the battleground language of "ifs" and "don'ts" (*if you don't stop, I'll...*), use "when-then" to matter-of-factly report what sound you CAN hear and CAN respond to.

Gram-meee, I want more pudding.

I cannot understand that *squeaky, whiny* sound.

When I hear Maya's regular voice **then** I can help Maya.

USE YOUR OWN VOICE TO DEMONSTRATE THE SOUND THAT *DOESN'T* WORK AND THE SOUND THAT *DOES* WORK

Make your own voice whine as you describe the whiny sound you cannot respond to. Then bring your voice down to it's normal tone as you describe the sound you *will* respond to.

Remember, we do not *decide* to whine. Your child may not even be aware she is doing it. Demonstrating the sounds will help her become aware.

Even with highly-developed language and abstract thinking skills, adults find it hard to accurately describe the sound of a whine, yet we all know it when we hear it. Let your child hear it.

HAVE A WHINING PARTY

Set a timer and have a short whining party. The whole family can join in. This will help your child understand what a whine sounds like and feels like. Also, on a day that seems full of whines, a whining party can provide a nice outlet. Often the energy will shift to laughter. In any case, if the party is set to a timer, everyone, especially the concrete thinking toddler, will know it is time to stop.

....

WHEN your child asks correctly be sure to respond *even if your answer is still No*.

ACKNOWLEDGE THE ACCOMPLISHMENT	HONOR THE THINKING AND NAME IT	RESPOND HONESTLY	HELP PROBLEM-SOLVE
You knew exactly how to ask mom.	You are thinking it would be a good idea to have a cookie.	This is a time when we don't have cookies. Remember, we have cookies after our sandwich.	You can have an apple! Come choose one. Watch me while I cut it up.
Children love the feeling of accomplishment. Even if he does not get what he wants, he does get your attention and support for mastery of a skill.	Putting words to his thought process supports language and problem-solving skills. It also supports his sense of self by confirming that he is a person who knows something about his own self.	A "No" delivered with empathy can lessen the frustration of being thwarted from what we want.	For example you can: • Offer an acceptable alternative • Make the temptation disappear • Use distraction

Whining is an all-ages behavior. Expect to reteach this lesson over and over again.

I DON'T WANNA!

WHINE AND CHEESE PARTY

How many times until he gets it?
Many. It's typical for whining to go away then come back strong during the pre-school years. Chances are good it will reappear in the teen years. Whining is a communication device we can use at any age. Eventually, we can learn to use it sparingly and appropriately. The good news is that determining "The Why of the Whine" becomes much easier as children grow.

When I whine back to teach what a whine sounds like, I feel like I'm mocking my child. Am I?
Toddlers don't understand sarcasm. But toddlers do understand anger, and they know when mom and dad are displeased. Check in with your head and heart. If you feel like you are mocking, rather than demonstrating, you may be harboring some anger and frustration. Your child can pick up on these negative responses.

We model the whine, not to retaliate, but to help them understand what it is that needs to change. It is a *big* challenge to not express irritation at a whine. Take a breath and remember that your child is not *trying* to whine to make life harder for you. She is learning to speak a new language and you are her (patient) teacher.

How do I stop yelling and screaming?
Like whining, yelling and screaming get our attention, and are another way to practice this powerful tool called "voice" and learn what all it can do. When a loud voice is used inappropriately, you can: 1) model the voice needed at that time; 2) use distraction to redirect the child to a new interest; 3) sing, for instance, if toddler decides to yell as baby is falling asleep, turning it into a favorite song can often make the sounds easier to modulate; and 4) if all else fails, remove the child (it may be helpful to explain the natural consequence, such as not having a favorite food because you had to leave the store early).

For **yelling**, we teach about *where* and *when* ("inside" and "outside" voices) while also understanding that it takes time to learn where and when to use loud sounds, whispers, and a general speaking voice.

Screaming is rooted in emotional or physical stress. It is not a time for teaching; it is a time for calming. See Meltdowns (p. 31) for helpful calming tools.

Caregiver Reminders:
- To whine is to recognize, on some level, that sound is powerful. This understanding can help expand interest in learning language.

- Sound is abstract. We cannot touch it, meet it, or hold it. Children are concrete learners. The statement "don't whine" is hard for a concrete learner to understand. The concrete learner needs to hear what a whine sounds like and what a normal voice sounds like.

TIPS TO STOP THE WHINING BEFORE IT STARTS

1 Sometimes a child will whine because other methods of getting attention have been ignored. This is why when your child makes a request in the way you want her to, even if you cannot say yes, it is important to respond so that she knows she has communicated successfully.

2 Whining is almost always a request for help. Behind that whiny sound is a belief: *Mom, I trust you to make this better for me*. At the root of a whine is a sense of powerlessness, and while it is true that toddlers have little ability to help themselves, giving them some control and choice when possible can help reduce the frustration that can lead to whining.

3 The ability to delay gratification can reduce the intensity of frustration that can, in turn, lead to behaviors such as whining. While it is developmentally *too much to ask* of a toddler to wait for extended periods of time, you can lay the groundwork for developing the skill of delayed gratification by "supporting the wait." This might mean that you spend time to talk the child through the "long" process of pouring their milk, or it might mean holding and comforting him as another child finishes playing with a toy. Perhaps you "support the wait" by engaging the child in helping to get things ready for her snack. You and your child will find strategies that best fit as verbal and social skills continue to develop and expand.

The Bumpy Day
Techniques to help smooth the day

Your time is at a premium. So in this section we put our advice in pictures to speed understanding, support clarity, and ease recall...but also to highlight facial expression and body language because: *We parent with our bodies.* Words are abstract. Your toddler benefits when your physical presence translates words into meaning and action.

Day-to-day our parenting bodies build:

Shared attention. We often wrap children in our arms to create focus, such as when we read together or when we want to teach or guide. In this way, our physical bodies create and maintain shared attention and support our leadership role.

Boundaries. Adult bodies help define boundaries for safe play and positive behavior. Arms will spread wide to create a safe corner for a child. One firmly placed arm can act like a railroad barrier, preventing a "snatch-and-run" of another child's toy. Sometimes, physical nearness itself is beneficial, as young ones seem to borrow from the steady presence of an adult.

Meaning. Body cues are often a child's most reliable source of information. Dad can tell his upset child that "everything is all right," but if dad's body is rigid, stressed, and agitated, the child gets the message: everything is *not* all right. In another example: Toddler is playing on the floor. Mom needs to tell him "it's time to go," so she (1) stands in the doorway and throws her words across the room; (2) stands nearby and says the words while looking at her smartphone; or (3) kneels down and says the words while making eye contact and perhaps even holding up a pair of shoes.

(1) and (2) ask too much of a toddler and set mom up for frustration. With (3), the child may resist, but now mom is dealing with a transition issue (using her transition tools). She is *not* dealing with a transition issue compounded and amplified by a communication issue.

The toddler years demand a lot of your parental time and energy. To also focus your attention on how you parent *physically* may feel to you like "one more thing" to add to your never-ending list of parental tasks. But, you may be surprised. When we know the value of bringing our bodies, not simply our words, to the task of child guidance, we can *reduce* the time and energy we spend correcting child behavior. So rather than "one more thing," think of it instead as a shortcut to improved communication.

Also, it can be helpful to remember that *small shifts make big differences*. The seven questions below can help nudge these shifts. Make it a habit to check in with each of them and it may smooth many of the bumps in your day.

1. **Do I have my child's attention before giving instructions?**

2. **Have I used "when... then..."?** (Remember that "ifs" and "don'ts" can invite a power struggle.)

3. **Have I reported the behavior the child needs to change?** (A simple description such as, "*I see a boy jumping on the sofa,*" will help bring his awareness to his behavior before you guide the change.)

4. **Have I created a mental picture of the positive behavior?** (It is more helpful to tell a child, "*Remember, you will do* [positive]," than to tell her, "*Don't do* negative]*!*")

5. **Have I planned our outings to fit my child's need for rest, food, and stimulation?**

6. **Have I looked at the outing through my child's eyes?**

7. **Have I taken care of myself?** (A rested and fed parent has more reserves to bring to the ebb and flow of a day.)

PART 3: EASING THE EVERYDAY

SUPPORTING SLEEP

Drowning in a Sea of Sleep Advice?

From solutions to steps to secrets, there is no shortage of advice on sleep. There are even sleep consultants that will, for a hefty price, take the night shift for you.

If you are hoping for a single beacon in this sea of sleep advice, we're sorry, we have no fixed set of coordinates to offer you. No one does.

This is because parenting is an art. Nurturing and loving children is just too important, interesting, intricate, enriching (and, yes, challenging) for any formula.

What we *do* have for you are oars, a sturdy boat, and a well-calibrated compass—the tools you need to successfully map the unique route that works for you and your family.

The subject of this chapter is sleep, but we all know that the real subject is *not sleeping*. Children go through phases of sleep difficulties. It's normal. Adults do, too. But when children are not sleeping, it can be particularly baffling. When this happens, it's always good to remember that though sleep is innate, it is not innately easy.

Sleep is a *biological imperative* and a *skill*, one that can take some time and practice for little bodies to figure out. Sleep has multiple components—biological, developmental, social—therefore it can be impacted by multiple sources—physical and emotional health, developmental milestones, even household rhythms and parent expectations.

SLEEP IS BIOLOGICAL

Most of us think the opposite of asleep is awake and the opposite of awake is asleep. Yet wakefulness and sleep are part of a continuum. But what does that mean?

It means that when we are awake, we may also be drifting to and further from states of sleep. It means that when we are asleep, we may also be drifting to and further from states of alertness. And, most importantly for you right now, it means that when we say a child has "slept through the night" what we really mean is that she has slept, lightly roused, settled back into sleep *on her own*, roused again, settled, etc.

The definition of "a good sleeper," then, is a child who is good at transitioning through the sleep cycle, without assistance.

You may remember your toddler as an infant repeatedly cycling through states of alertness and states of sleep. You very likely supported and eased your baby's transitions through these states. For instance, you may remember:

- **Quiet sleep:** This is the deep sleep when a parent can trim toenails without rousing the baby. The baby may make sucking movements or twitch, but there is no face or eye movement.

Toddler Sleep

On average, toddlers need about 12–14 hours of sleep in a 24-hour period.

Often around 18 months, they begin to settle into one nap a day lasting anywhere from 1–3 hours.

- **Active sleep:** Active sleep has body and face movements. It is a state that can more easily move to arousal or may result in resettling and additional quiet sleep.

- **Drowsy:** Sometimes called the "two blink" state because of the heavy-lidded slow blinking, this is the state in which parents are encouraged to place their babies in the crib to "learn to go to sleep on their own." Dull or glazed eyes can also be a sign of drowsiness.

- **Quiet Alert:** Characterized by a bright open look, this is when it is easiest for the baby to focus and enjoy being with the family.

- **Active Alert:** This state is moving towards overwhelm. The eyes are less bright and the baby indicates much more sensitivity to noise and hunger.

- **Crying:** This state tells you the baby has had more than enough. In addition to crying and a grimace there is a lot of disorganized body movement.

Though you may not be consciously aware of it, you likely already have expert knowledge of your *toddler's* pattern of cycling through drowsy, quiet, and active sleep states. In fact, sleep support is probably embedded into your schedule (though you may think of it as "tantrum avoidance"). The proof: You know the best time to run errands and the best window for your toddler's lunch and dinner.

You may also have become sensitive to your toddler's unique cues. One clear signal some parents report is an otherwise able walker who begins to fall or trip more frequently (even small bumps seem to hurt more when a child is tired). For some, the signal is a cranky child. For others, it might be a suddenly hyperactive child.

So while you cannot control your child's (or anyone's) sleep—**you do have a great deal of control over the sleep schedule and your own sensitivity to your child's cues.**

SLEEP IS DEVELOPMENTAL

Colds, allergies, physical discomfort can disrupt sleep, but so can developmental milestones. For infants, teething and even learning to sit up or pulling up to stand may trigger a disruption.

For toddlers, separation anxiety triggered by social-emotional development can bring distress to the sleep routine. After all, **nighttime is a very long stretch to be alone** and separated from parents.

For older toddlers, fear can create new nighttime challenges. With the expansion of language and a more active imagination at play, a child once comfortable in a darkened room can become actively resistant to sleep now that he has the ability to scare himself with his imagination.

SLEEP IS SOCIAL

Stories, snuggles, tucking in, the feeling you have as you watch your child drift off, these are all elements of the social components of sleep. As young children grow and imaginations develop along with verbal skills, children will often begin to engage parents in an attempt to expand and extend the social component to sleep.

You may experience this as the *"One More"* phenomenon—that is, *one more* hug, *one more* kiss, *one more* story, etc.

Cultural traditions, family values, physical space, and family resources will determine the social structure around sleep. But whether bedrooms are shared or whether work schedules create unique circumstances, remember that **your choice for supporting and guiding sleep should function well for the child *and* you *and* the whole family.**

For example, some families have extended bedtime rituals and routines that keep child and parent together until the child sleeps. Using *The Test of 3* (does it function well for the child and you and the whole family), this choice may pass the test if, for instance, it takes the pressure off the child, it is satisfying for both parent

Screen Time & Sleep

There is increasing evidence that the light from screen time (TV, computers, phones, iPads, etc.) within an hour of bedtime will make it difficult to transition to sleep.

For smoother sleep transitions, it will be helpful to find other ways to calm and settle your child.

and child, and is short enough in duration to not negatively impact other family needs.

However, if the child is happy, but the individual parent feels "trapped" or it causes too much disruption for siblings, couple time, or conflicts with other family values, this choice needs adjusting (see "Changing the Sleep Routine" below).

WINDING DOWN TO SUPPORT SLEEP

The better-rested child sleeps better. Overtired children are more susceptible to being overwhelmed, which increases the potential for meltdowns and decreases the brain's ability to be flexible, making it much harder to interact smoothly with others.

When a child does not transition into sleep during the natural biological window, stress hormones signal the body to pull on survival reserves, triggering a kind of "second wind." Some energetic children will consistently push themselves past this window to the point of exhaustion.

Parents may find that romping with a toddler prior to bedtime is joyful, but may also get in the way of winding down for sleep. Starting the sleep routine earlier and at a pace that is not hurried can help. Don't give up the joyful romping! But do find a time for it that supports positive closure to the day for everyone.

CHANGING THE SLEEP ROUTINE

Before entering into any significant change to the bedtime routine, it is helpful to begin with the strategies that best support your child in other transitions.

In the chapter on transitions (p. 35) we talk about how the pre-telling of events (also called *oral rehearsal*) can help anchor the toddler in the day. We can pre-tell the new story of bedtime at an earlier point in the day. It may sound something like this:

> *I noticed that you like it best when daddy stays in your room until you go to sleep. Did you know*

A consistent sleep schedule, well-recognized routines, loving rituals, and an awareness of what calms your unique child will help to ease bedtime struggles.

that when people are three years old part of their growing-up work is to practice going to sleep on their own after their teeth are brushed and the story is over?

Tonight when story time with daddy is over, he will give you his extra big nighttime hug and turn on your fairy tale tape so you can listen to them as many times as you need to. You can pick which one you want to listen to first.

When beginning a new routine or implementing a change (such as: move to own room, own bed, or falling asleep alone) **follow-through and consistency are going to be the keys to success.**

To make sure you can remain committed, **avoid choosing a method that in your heart feels wrong**—no matter how much your friend or that TV psychologist raves about it.

When you need to shift a sleep clock it is best done gradually. For an earlier bedtime, begin bedtime rituals 15 minutes earlier every night, repeating until the desired bedtime is reached.

Also, because the body (circadian rhythm) is impacted by daylight, playing outside in the morning is another way to help children set their internal clock.

Remember that change takes time, but also remember that change *does* happen.

You may just find that what seemed impossible on night #1 can begin working on night #4.

On the following page is a list of general guidelines you can use to support your child as he or she develops and manages the skill of sleep.

- **Regular Bedtime & Wake Time**
  Consistent sleep and wake times allow the body's natural rhythms to develop. [This applies to daytime naps, too.]

- **Routines & Rituals**
  The bedtime routine plays an important role in signaling the body and the brain to prepare for sleep, while also helping the child to feel secure.

  The routine should include all the steps for bedtime, such as tooth brushing, jammies, etc., but also rituals that create a positive association with sleep, such as story- and snuggle-time.

- **Objects**
  Loveys, such as a stuffed animal or blanket, can be great company at night. Other types of objects (that are safe for beds) can also create a connection to mom and dad. One example is mom's (or dad's) sweater that holds her (or his) scent.

  Perhaps, mom will tightly hug the object and offer it as *"full of mama's hugs if you need one during the night."*

  Also, a soft, safe photo book filled with family pictures can help a child feel connected during the long nighttime separation.

- **Figuring out what YOUR child needs**
  What soothes one person may excite another. What eases fear in one may spark it in another. Whatever worked like a charm for your sister-in-law or your favorite TV host, may not work for you. You'll know best what works for you and your child. For instance:

  ### Silence or Sound?
  Parents are often advised to "create a quiet environment." But some children actually become more keyed up in the quiet, and may benefit from music, a recorded story, or an open door that keeps them connected to the bustling sounds of the household. To find out what is best for your child, watch her throughout the day, paying attention to how she responds to silence and to sound.

  ### Defense or Distraction?
  Some children like having a "monster spray" by their bed, yet for others this kind of defensive tool may be a constant reminder of monsters, stoking their anxiety. Does a spray bottle or flashlight reassure your child? Or, does he do better with stories that comfort him, such as a tale of a dream he will have filled with all things that are comforting and safe? You can also record a favorite story and he may listen to it as many times as he needs to help him sleep.

  ### Look for Clues.
  Pay attention to how your child treats stuffed animals and/or dolls. Sometimes she can show you what she needs by how she tucks in her own toys.

TALKING TOILETING

Does a comment have you feeling criticized?

Think of it this way: They are expressing their own sense of accomplishment, not judging you.

Share in their success:
"I'm glad it worked for your Susie."

Acknowledge difference:
"I'm sure it is different for moms who are with their children all day."

Stand behind your healthcare provider:
"My doctor says George isn't showing any signs that he is ready yet. Every child is different."

Agree to think about it:
"Thanks, I'll give it some thought" (of course, you get to decide just how much thought...)

F or most parents, "potty-training" is the most daunting of the major milestones. It's not hard to find advice, whether from books, websites, the wisdom of family and friends, or any of the endless electronic forums that discuss and promote various theories and strategies. Because toileting challenges can vary, it's certainly useful to have so many resources to turn to, yet, to get the most help (and the least confusion), it's important to equip yourself before diving in—and that is the purpose of this chapter.

We focus on the basics of the toileting process and its challenges, so that you can be purposeful in your approach, have a grounding from which to problem-solve, and make the most use of (or politely discard) the various strategies, tips, and advice you'll encounter along the way.

TOILET TRAINING VS. TOILET LEARNING

"All my children were toilet trained by the time they were one-year old."

When you hear these words, or something similar, you know that you are in the realm of **TOILET TRAINING**. Testimonies such as these typically come from the generations that parented before the age of disposable diapers, and they may indeed be true. After all, washing machines and dryers were not the standard they are today. Imagine how motivated mothers were (again, remembering the times, it *was* almost always mothers) to have their children beyond diapers as quickly as possible. So, while Toilet Training was indeed practiced early...

...the one "trained" was more often the mother than the child.

Mothers would watch their children for any body cues. They would spend significant time entertaining their baby as he or she was seated on the potty chair so that the immediate success could be reinforced. Mothers may also have read the early works of Dr. Spock who, at that phase of his understanding, taught that children

One of the most common pitfalls is asking a child: **"Do you have to go to the bathroom?"** or "**Do you** *want* **to go to the bathroom?"**

Young children are very concrete thinkers. "Have to" and "Want to" are easily answered with a "No."

Once a child has said "No," the parent is in the awkward position of trying to convince the child that "Yes" is the right answer.

live to the clock. Therefore, children were fed at the same time every day and mothers could learn about and predict when to place their child on the potty chair.

Today we encourage parents to support their children in **TOILET LEARNING**, so that success is not centered in the mother's training, but in the child who is learning about:

- the body
- the language of the task
- the family expectations about self care
- the motor skills to get to the bathroom and manage clothes
- how to pay attention to internal cues
- how to prioritize internal cues so that they override the desire to play

Is it any wonder that when children have all these tasks to integrate that the age of toilet learning may range from 18 months to 4 years?

LEARNING *ABOUT* COMES BEFORE LEARNING *HOW*

Signs of readiness (see pp. 60–61) will help you know when to start practicing Toilet Learning, but from very early on you set the groundwork by:

- Using the vocabulary of toileting
- Using positive language (avoid "you're dirty" "icky poo")
- Reinforcing the fact that everyone poops and pees
- Reporting cues when you see them ("Your body wants to go pee")
- Encouraging good associations with diaper changes (special toy, songs, etc.)
- Changing diapers when needed so the child does not get used to the wet feeling

- Sharing how the bathroom and toilet function (you can dump and flush diaper poo to show that the toilet is where it goes)

- Encouraging positive associations with the potty chair: introduce it as belonging to the child; decorating it or sitting on it while playing are both fine

CHILDREN LEARN FROM WATCHING

As adults we don't use the restroom because we *want to*. We use the restroom because we are aware of our internal body cues. We *listen to our body*. We can help our children with this major developmental milestone, when we are *overt* about "listening to our bodies."

For example, if you are doing dishes you can report aloud that your body is telling you that it is time to use the restroom. If you are watching an enjoyable TV program, you can report aloud that you are listening to your body and you are going to go to the bathroom and then hurry back to your program (in doing so, you are modeling leaving an engaging activity for self care). If you can place the program on hold, then you can model how we are able to have our "play wait for us" until we return.

As you support and encourage your child, keep in mind that **successful toilet learning is dependent on the child reading his or her own body cues and responding with self care**. The child's body awareness is a major milestone toward successful integration of this life skill.

WHEN TO START

The questions on the next page will help you determine your child's readiness. Remember that, should you begin, but then find it is simply not working, it is okay to stop and try again later. This shouldn't be interpreted as a failure. Parents are the family "spin doctors" who will help to make meaning of events surrounding little ones. Use language of success (not praise) to recognize successful steps toward the goal and report that someday very soon she will be using the bathroom just like mom and dad.

There's No One Way

There are children who quickly learn motor skills, but focus so deeply on their other interests that awareness of body cues takes longer.

There are children who are so aware of internal cues or are so distressed by wet or soiled diapers that they quickly associate using the potty chair with comfort, yet have "accidents" as they struggle to manage all the mechanics of clothing.

There are children who are so socially aware of the task that they will hide (find a private space) at the first body cue rather than seek out an adult for help.

As your child's teacher and coach through this learning process there are **3 Questions** to consider before beginning the actual practice of Toilet Learning.

The answers to these questions will not only help you *gauge* your child's readiness, they will direct you towards *specific avenues of support* to help build your child's readiness.

> You can answer Yes to more than one question. Multiple Yes answers simply give you multiple avenues of support.

Does your child consistently wake up dry from a nap?

This question helps to determine if your little one has enough bladder capacity to stay dry for a couple of hours.

If yes...

For a child who consistently wakes dry, the entry into toilet learning is **positive exposure and reinforcement.** Books are a great tool for this. At your local library, you should be able to find picture books all about the fact that every animal goes potty: kittens and puppies, elephants and tigers, and even moms and dads!

> *...And you know what? As you grow you will be able to do this too. Your body is showing you that you're growing on the inside just like you keep growing bigger on the outside.*

Dolls and stuffed animals can also reinforce the practice...

> *...Do you think dolly knows about going potty? Do you think you can teach her?*

Then, you create opportunity: the wake up ritual now includes a potty stop...

> *...just like mom and dad...*

Does your child signal awareness of internal cues?

A child who hides or chooses a favorite private location for bowel movements is responding to an internal cue, signaling some level of body awareness.

If yes...

For the child who exhibits some awareness of his internal cues, the entry to support toilet learning is to **report to the child what his body is telling him**, and to share the information that when his body tells him to go to a private place, "the private place" is the bathroom.

> *...One day pretty soon you will be able to put it in the potty just like mom and dad do when our bodies tell us it's time.*

At this point, it will help the child to make the association if all diapers are changed in the bathroom.

Admittedly, this may be tough for those accustomed to changing their very active little one in a variety of rooms in the home.

Does your child show social interest in toileting?

Children with social interest will look forward to the new clothes, the equipment, being in charge of flushing, engaging in hand washing, and other elements that surround the toileting task.

If yes...

For the child with social interest, use language that helps her to understand that...

> *...these are things people do as part of their growing up.*

If there is significant social interest but little ability to read internal cues then a loving adult leader may be able to help them by **practicing** when the child is most likely to be successful: upon awakening, 15-20 minutes after a meal or significant drink, or immediately before entering a bath.

One note of warning: These children will want to wear their big kid clothes perhaps before they are fully ready. You may support your child by letting them know that while people learn they need to practice. Then schedule brief practice times of wearing big-kid clothes during the day. If the child has an accident simply clean it up and let them know that they can practice again tomorrow. Reassure the child:

> *One day pretty soon you will remember to go into the bathroom, even when you are busy playing.*

Practice time is a great strategy for preventing multiple accidents in one day, which otherwise can create a learning climate of repeat failures and increase parental stress.

SOME FACTS ABOUT TOILET LEARNING
(TO HELP YOU STAY PATIENT AND UNDERSTANDING)

- This skill takes time to learn. It may take one month. It may take three. Don't ask one child to be like another.

- Daytime dryness typically comes before nighttime dryness.

- Children may experience "regression" when life changes (weather, trips, new baby, etc.) especially if the skill has been newly mastered.

- Bladder control and bowel control may or may not happen at the same time.

- Children respond to support. Do not force him to sit on the potty. Be sympathetic and straightforward about accidents, reminding that it takes time and he will be successful soon.

- One way to start is just by practicing sitting on the potty. If you can, arrange those practice times to coincide with times the child is more likely to need to go, such as soon after waking up, or 20 minutes or so after a meal.

- It's fine for the child to look at a book while on the potty. It can allow muscles the opportunity to respond naturally without the pressure to perform.

- It's okay to use small rewards, but keep them simple (sticker charts to show their success, for instance). It's also okay to use games. Some little ones will enjoy sitting through brief songs and finger plays. Games that involve aiming for a target may boost the motivation of little boys.

- Be aware that if boys are more often in the care of women, they benefit less from adult modeling. You may want to be intentional about offering more opportunities to model behavior for him.

- Be aware that children may have fears related to bowel movements. Imagine if you didn't know how bodies work what you might think or feel if you sat on a toilet and a part of your body fell off? If your child seems frightened, focus on security. Sometimes, wearing the diaper on the potty chair can help as a transition.

- Be positive and encouraging but avoid overdoing the praise. It can be overwhelming and make the child feel as though she has to do it perfectly every time.

- If it's just not working, it's okay to stop and try again at a later time.

- At the same time, avoid putting it off and starting late. Some children may not be ready until they are 3 1/2 and older, but these are the exceptions. Having developmentally appropriate expectations for your child is central to his overall well-being.

- In the case of repeated and on-going toileting resistance in the older toddler, consult your pediatrician. Constipation and allergies may be playing a role. In even older children, it may have entered into the realm of a power struggle, which your doctor should be able to help identify.

- One resource that offers clear and concise information on toileting is the Pediatric Advisor A-Z at childrenshealthnetwork.org.

MANAGING MEALTIME

You've probably heard about the benefits of the shared family meal. Recent research suggests that eating together has a positive effect on language development, as well as nutrition, it even seems to protect against risky adolescent behavior. Plus, we humans just seem to like to "break bread" together. From birth, food has a social component—dads of newborns are often very aware of the power of shared meals to support attachment, especially if they feel they cannot engage fully with the feeding process. And this social component continues across the life span. If you think about it, those people you know best are those with whom you share meals.

However, take this idealized notion of the shared family meal off the page and into the dining room of a family with young children who won't eat, or won't sit still, or get "creative" with food and you might wonder how it is that family mealtime can be so beneficial.

The reality: many adults find dinner with kids to be stressful, even unpleasant, and battles over food are quite common. But, families can address some of the barriers to a positive mealtime, take a bit of that pressure off, and lay the groundwork for a continued positive relationship with food and with one another.

In this chapter we offer you some general mealtime strategies, information that will help you avoid power struggles over food, and also specific suggestions for common mealtime dilemmas.

MEALTIME STRATEGIES

Keep it short. Toddlers have a developmental drive to move. Sitting still for any amount of time can be very difficult for early walkers and climbers so have their food fully ready before confining the child to the high chair.

Waiting for you as you run back and forth to the refrigerator spends precious moments of the "still time" they have available to eat and engage with you.

Also, while you and older members of the family may enjoy lingering at the table, this is developmentally difficult for a toddler.

It is okay if they play on the floor or with a toy or art materials at the table while you continue your dinner.

Keep them company. It can be tempting to put food in front of your child and get something else done while they eat. Instead, create a positive context for meals by talking with her, sharing bites when appropriate, and, at the same time, give yourself a moment to be unhurried in your day.

Keep it colorful and fun. Kiwi eyes, a carrot nose, and an apple slice for a mouth: "Dressing up" food is an effective way to get kids to eat. Parents have known this forever. Now it is backed up by research.*

HOW TO AVOID THE POWER STRUGGLE

The basic formula sounds easy: The parent is responsible for providing nutritionally-sound food. The child is responsible for eating (and choosing how much). The end.

Yet, anyone who has nurtured a child from infancy knows that food is deeply connected to love. As a parent, you were once solely responsible for feeding your infant. Now, your child is becoming responsible for feeding himself. That is a huge transition (for both of you!).

Because we want our children to have the best nutrition, because we want them to grow and thrive, **we can easily get into a dynamic of pushing or withholding food**.

Yet, too much pushing and withholding can inadvertently lead to a relationship with food that is less about nutrition and more about struggle, power, control, and, sometimes, solace. To help take you out of the food battle, keep these six points in mind:

*Zampollo, F. Acta Paediatrica, January 2012. Cornell University.

6 Points to Keep in Mind...

1. Research shows that when left to make their own choices children will, over time, eat in a way that is nutritionally balanced.

2. Each meal does not have to be nutritionally "perfect." It is what is eaten over the course of a day—some pediatricians suggest over the course of a week—that matters. So, if on Tuesday your toddler is on a cereal kick, remember that it can be balanced with other essential nutrients on Thursday.

3. Understanding portion size can help you resist the urge to "push" food. In general, a serving size is one measured tablespoon per age of child. How many chunks of green bean can actually fit in a measured tablespoon? Two, maybe three? When your toddler eats four bites of green bean she has probably eaten an amount appropriate to her age and size. Further, you may find that when portions are kept small it is easier for the child to focus, rather than be distracted by the science of mixing and smearing all the food before them.

4. Understand that your child may have his own internal eating clock. He may love a big breakfast and lighter fare for dinner. Or, he may not be ready for very much food until mid-morning. Noticing and planning your offerings to match your child's preferences can create a more positive relationship with food.

5. Expect fluctuations. When a child is in a growth spurt everything about serving size and interest in food can shift. Some days it may seem your child packs away more food than you! In the absence of power struggles over food, trust her body to eat what it needs to maintain the energy she needs.

6. Be aware of alternative sources of nutrition. For instance, for the child not yet ready to handle the textures of meat, try mashed up beans or cubes of tofu for protein. You can find other alternatives for nutrients on the USDA.gov website.

SHIFTING THE PATTERN

While keeping these six points in mind can help you make good decisions about how to engage your child with food, if a push-resist pattern is already in place or if food has been a successful way to engage mom and dad, what else can you do to shift the pattern?

- **Turn the battleground into a playground**: Invite your child to have fun with food. This can mean dressing food up—putting raisin eyes on pear halves, or cutting food into fun shapes—and it can mean games—go ahead and have the broccoli-helicopter fly into the mouth, or encourage a story the child can act out—*"That pea looks brave and adventurous. I think it wants to explore the cave first."* The possibilities are endless.

- **Make a food chart**: There is something about charts and children. Children love the "I did it!" feeling and charts can make an accomplishment tangible and visual. Plus, there are all those fun stickers and smiley faces. An I'm-Trying-New-Foods Chart can help motivate a child to taste new things. Make the goal easy: Try one new food a week—just a taste—you may find the child wants to try more.

- **Engage your child in the process of making food**: Children are more likely to try what they have helped to make, plus, they get the added good feeling of being capable and helpful. Some of the world's most renowned chefs have fond memories of being invited at a young age into the kitchen to explore and contribute.

SOME SPECIFIC CONCERNS

Some sociologists have suggested that **food resistance** served as a protective factor in early hunter-gatherer cultures. "Baby proofing" the environment for dangerous edibles would have been impossible; a toddler's active resistance could help keep her alive. In our current environment, your calm offering coupled with modeling a positive approach to food will provide a pathway for your child as she moves beyond this usually brief stage.

Foods that I Tried

	YUM!	SO-SO	I'LL TRY IT AGAIN SOMEDAY
carrots	✔		
chicken			✔
soup		✔	
quinoa		✔	

Allergies: a growing concern

Food allergy symptoms can range from itchy skin, mucus or bloody stools, an inability to calm to life-threatening breathing problems, and more.

Short of an immediate crisis reaction to a food, when an intolerance or allergy is suspected, parents and the family doctor may need to engage in a multi-week process to identify the suspect food.

For the very youngest, this may require maintaining a food diary and recording not only the kind and amount of food, but possible reactions to the food—including behavior changes.

Textures that invite or repel may be another factor in feeding young children. Notice if your child responds differently to dry or smooth textures. Children have preferences, just as some adults resist the skin on peaches and for others it is a non-issue.

It may be that very small chunks of cheese will be better received than milk or yogurt, or vice versa. Canned kidney or chickpeas (rinsed to remove excess salt) may be more satisfying for your finger-food eater than equal portions of meats, which require much more chewing and tongue control.

Throwing food may be the signal that your child is finished eating. It may also be a way to engage the important adults in their life.

If you are hoping for adult conversation during a meal with a toddler, you and the other adult may be frustrated. As your child develops more language and positive ways to engage in adult interaction you may be able to add more interaction time with your co-parent. For now, it is often easier to plan for adult time after your little one is in bed.

Table manners and the rules for spoons and forks will develop over the preschool years. Again, as language becomes more functional and fine motor skills develop, children will begin to demonstrate their awareness of the social rules of life.

You may find your language and family patterns echoed in your toddler's kitchen play, or with dolls, or in collaborative play with peers. Teaching manners like please and thank you, turn taking, and appropriate use of spoons, forks, and dull spreading tools will become of interest to your active learner. You may find yourself invited to more tea parties than you imagined!

Today's efforts will help you tomorrow

As your toddlers grow into kids, the social pressure of friends may impact their interest in food. Adding to peer influences will be the demands of after school events, music lessons, and sports schedules. The traditions you set now can help with future challenges, as will keeping in mind the strategies that worked best when your child was younger.

You can maintain a positive relationship with food and with one another by continuing to block time for shared meals and conversations.

An occasional hurried or missed family meal is to be expected, but the gift of maintaining a shared family table can last a lifetime.

THE PLAYDATE GUIDE

Play*date* or Play*group*

Because playdates for young children tend to be group events, many scenarios in this chapter include multiple children. Nonetheless, almost everything shared here will also apply to one-on-one play.

P laydates offer wonderful stimulation for young children and much needed adult conversation for parents. Yet, playdates can often end in tears and meltdowns, leaving mom and dad to wonder how something that sounds so fun can end up being so stressful. The good news: **a bit of planning and preparation can help ease the eruptions and conflicts that can often accompany playdates.**

More good news: A great way to make sure your *toddler's* playdates are successful is to meet your own needs to be social by scheduling your own no-kids-allowed *grown-up* playdates.

RECIPE FOR TEARS

For *children*, playdates are full of both *lots* and *new*—lots of kids, lots of big people, lots of noise, stuff, and activity, plus new things, places, animals, toys, and rules.

For *parents*, playdates can test our need for balance, as we try to make up for a deficit of adult company in our lives, while the needs of children literally tug at our shirtsleeves.

For *children*, playdates can present a big challenge: *sharing* (we will nudge you to call this "*taking turns*").

For *parents*, playdates can present other challenges: parenting under the watchful eyes of others and disciplining other people's children.

SWAP IN SOME MORE HEALTHY INGREDIENTS

Certain ingredients can make for a more successful playdate. Some will be more essential to the mix than others, depending on temperament, circumstance, and more. Some are under your control. Some are not. **And like asking a neighbor for a cup of sugar, for some ingredients you may need to reach out to others.**

Main Ingredient

The most important ingredient for a successful playdate is **YOU**. Playing well with others demands the ability to negotiate, to be safe, and to honor ownership. No one under age 4 should be expected to do any of this without adult support. Besides increasing safety and reducing conflict, your involvement helps model and teach these skills.

Other Ingredients

Manageable Numbers: There is no magic number, but six kids plus six adults in one living room is a lot. For a less stimulating environment, some playgroups split into subgroups.

Neutral Turf: Sometimes just being on neutral turf, like a playground, can reduce conflict. Finding appropriate indoor space can be a challenge, though libraries sometimes have play areas or rooms that can be reserved.

Limited Duration: Quite often one hour is enough for young children. Rarely, is one hour enough for adults. If sticking to a short time frame proves difficult, it is doubly important to stay sensitive to "signs" that children are becoming overwhelmed (see next).

Watch for Signs: Because the company of adult friends is fun and may feel in short supply, parents tend to be reactive rather than proactive at playdates. As adults engage in conversation, early signs of trouble tend to be ignored.

To avoid eruptions, stay sensitive to signs, such as a child who begins to stick a little tighter, perhaps dropping in your lap more frequently, or play that has become disorganized, bodies that bump, crash, and fall more often. The child may be minimally refreshed with a hug, snack, or drink to give yourself a bit of transition time as you prepare to leave.

Prepare: Talk about the arrival—who is hosting and who will be there. Create a positive picture of how the child will behave:

> *Our friends Sam and Chloe are coming to play. Remember you have enough cars so everyone can drive.*

Also talk about what will happen when it is time to go:

> *We will sing our clean-up song when it is time for our friends to be ready to go home.*

Other Ingredients *(continued)*

Ease Arrival: Be purposeful. Even gregarious personalities can sometimes use help integrating into a new environment. Report what you see and demonstrate how to engage in this new place.

> *I see four of your friends sitting on the floor. Tami is building a train track ... looks like Sam is drawing. There are some toys in the corner. Let's go explore...*

Ease Departure: Again, be purposeful. Crisp departures are usually best. ***Say your goodbyes first***, then report to your child that you are leaving, ***gather her up and go*** (use your goodbye game or leaving ritual if you have one). If you linger at the door chatting, your child will get wound up again. To ease departure, use your best transition tools (see p. 35).

If you are the host, have an escape valve prepared ahead of time (it is much harder to be tactful and polite in the urgency of the moment). This can be a simple statement, such as:

> *This has been great, but it's time we brought it to a close. I can see that my Katie is overdue for a nap.*

Honor Temperament: Some children are quick to approach novelty; some are more measured in their approach. Some jump in; some will first observe. To support the child who needs more time,

arrive early so that instead of entering a big group, the group grows around him. Also, let him know it is okay to watch for a while.

He should feel you are a safe place for him, but be mindful of the difference between honoring temperament and rewarding withdrawal (if you are snack or attention central, it will be harder for him to join others).

Some children problem-solve verbally; some will use their bodies. If there is potential for grabbing, biting, or hitting, your support is to be close by (see *shadowing* on page 71) to assist and model problem-solving before it becomes physical.

Communicate with Other Parents: Contract with one another:

> *Jane and I will take swing duty, you two take the bench and enjoy each other. We'll switch in 15...*

It can also be helpful to share with others what you are working on with your child (i.e., turn-taking, hitting, etc.) so that other parents can be mindful of your goals (and you of theirs).

Schedule your own playdate: Grant yourself the permission to connect with others, be social, and enjoy friends without little ones underfoot and without guilt. Remember, ***there is zero correlation between self-denial and good mothering.*** Plan your own playdate. At your child's playdate, she's going to need you.

PEER PLAY: 4 STRATEGIES

With these four strategies you can help toddlers learn to have positive social interactions that meet their own needs and also maintain a safe and happy environment for everyone.

❶ Support turn taking:

- When you share a cookie with a friend, the cookie disappears. When you take turns on a tricycle, the tricycle comes back. This is why with young children, whenever possible, **we like to say** *taking turns* **rather than** *sharing.*

- Whatever rules for turn-taking are established (for ex: time limits or no time limits) they apply as much to the host as the guest. In other words, the child does not have to give up a toy she is playing with to another child just because that child is the guest.

- Don't force the rules of turn taking if all is fine. If Josie takes Lily's toy but Lily doesn't seem to mind, there's no need to force Josie to return it. But do reinforce the rule with your words:

   It looks like Lily is done with that, it's okay to have your turn now.

Likewise, if a child has waited for his turn successfully, but meanwhile became engaged in something else, you can acknowledge his success by simply reporting:

   Your turn is ready. Do you want the truck now? You can keep playing with the balls if you want to...

❷ Support respect for boundaries:

- When it comes to "stuff," we often have higher expectations of our children than we do of ourselves. Few of us would hand over our car keys to a new acquaintance or very easily let a friend borrow our laptop; **your child should not be expected to share her very favorite toys.** Chose a number—not too big—that your child may claim as "favorite toys" that can be put away. Then gently remind her that the rest of the toys are for everyone to take turns with.

- Adults don't (typically) share their spouses, children shouldn't be asked to share their loveys. But unlike the favorite toy that is put away, **children *can* keep their lovey nearby** during playdates (they can be a helpful anchor in challenging situations). But because a lovey is a boundary to be respected and honored, you will have to help should it get into other hands. For example, if another child takes it, you can say:

   You know what? That is Jerry's special friend and we keep it just for Jerry.

Then, redirect to another toy. To make it work, you may need to get in the play for a bit as well:

   I wonder if you have met Tulliver yet? I think he is in this box. Do you want to see what kind of animal Tulliver is?

❸ Support physical safety—*shadow*:

- Shadowing is staying physically near as your child attempts to play with other children.

- Close shadowing is essential for toddlers who bite, push, or hit—both for safety and to ensure that the behavior does not become a habit.

- Shadowing can take many forms.

- It may mean simply being close enough to sense, head-off, or respond to conflicts.

- It may involve becoming a temporary playmate:

   You know what? That ball is too big and fast for your friend. Let's play catch over here.

- It may involve actually entering into group play to help with negotiations.

- Sometimes shadowing will mean physically placing your body between children to maintain safety.

- When shadowing, stay mindful of your body language. It is very different to be in the presence of high alert, as opposed to calm attentiveness. By being aware of our own body messages we are able to reassure our intuitive learners that they are safe and supported.

❹ Support *reading* others' intentions:

- Young children cannot predict the intent of another. So when Thomas is playing and Susie enters, sees him and comes running over, Thomas may very well look scared and grab up his toy. To support Thomas's social skills and a positive interaction with Susie, use your words to give meaning to the other child's intent. Report what is happening and make statements about the approaching child's positive intent:

   Your friend Susie is coming to see what you are doing.

If you sense a budding conflict, you might say:

   Susie likes to see how the train works, too. Is this a time you can show her?

If there is an unwelcome grab for the train, statements such as...

   It looks like Susie isn't remembering the rule...

...will be more successful than "Susie, Give that back." Then, you may help direct Susie to another related toy or activity or help the children enter into turn-taking negotiations.

DISCIPLINING OTHER CHILDREN

When another parent is not anticipating or responding to their child's behavior, it is *always* okay to make the decision to keep your child safe. **Health, safety, and personal values are non-negotiable.**

Your whole spirit is impacted when you believe something and let it get trampled on. So if a visiting toddler is pulling the leaves off your philodendron or repeatedly yelling into your child's ear, do not think twice about stepping in. This may mean physically placing your body between your child and whatever dynamic is going on. It may mean confirming the rule (*"You know what? In our house..."*).

Remember that **to discipline is to teach.** So with other children use tones that will be helpful for the child:

> *You know what? Sam doesn't like to be pushed. It's not safe to push a friend. You can use your words to tell him you need a turn.*

PARENTING UNDER THE EYES OF OTHERS

Remember that as parents of toddlers **you and the other adults at the playgroup have more in common than not.** But if you are feeling on the spot, judged, or uncomfortable, it can be helpful to ask yourself why. Is the judgment real or assumed? Does the attention you feel come from empathy or interest, rather than criticism? Sometimes you can check: With a spirit of discovery ask other parents, *"Do you think there might be a better way?"* or *"Do you know anything that might help me with this?"*

If you do feel as if your parenting is under review, do your best not to let it tap your needed reserves and divert your attention away from your toddler. Visualize a protective bubble around you and your child or imagine that every eye on you is offering support. Self-efficacy and self-confidence will grow as you experience your own success with this new important and complicated task called raising a toddler.

What do I do when my child ignores his friend?

A child will sometimes retreat and refuse to play. In groups, this is not usually a problem (you can leave early or, if he is happy enough simply let him be). But, one-on-one and especially at a drop-off playdate or babysitting trade, this situation can be challenging for the adult in charge.

The reason a child retreats may be a mood or physical irritation; quite often the child is simply confused by a different temperament or confusing way of playing and just doesn't know what to do. So when George is sitting on the staircase and his guest Jack is playing alone and looking sad, you can:

- Say to Jack (so that George can overhear):

  > *You know what? It looks like George is not ready to play yet, I will play with you and George will join us when he is ready.*

- Get out something fun, usually this is something tactile, like playdoh or a sinkful of bubbles, and George is likely to find it irresistible.

When you take the pressure to perform off the child, quite often you can turn this situation around.

RITUALS & ROUTINES

We use "**ROUTINES**" as shorthand for "**RITUALS & ROUTINES**"—but only because it keeps things simple. We really do mean both. Though similar, in that both refer to something that is repeated, one refers to what that act is (*recurring, expected*) and the other to what that act creates (*meaning*). A kiss and hug signal bedtime. A kiss and hug mean, "I love you."

For most adults, the day is full of routines and rituals. Though often we become aware of them only when they are disrupted—by traffic snarls, for example, or a change of schedule. While a routine-filled life may not sound exciting, these repeated activities create a useful roadmap for our day and free us from having to focus on every small detail of living.

For toddlers who, as we learned in Chapter 1, live in a state of constant exploration and newness, routines and rituals are especially important. **Not only do they ease the day, they help build trust and support learning.**

ABOUT ROUTINES

Routines serve as mile markers on a day's path. At any age, the transition from sleep to waking can be disorienting. Many toddlers will make this transition three times over the course of one day. Familiar signals—wake up routines—will help anchor the child.

Maybe with the *first waking* of the day comes that extra snuggle with dad, then the diaper change (where that favorite toy is always waiting). Then food, followed by the car seat and the song mom always sings on the way to daycare.

The *second waking* is with friends, sharing smiles and words, followed by lunch and busy time.

The *third waking* comes with a smile from teacher, then a diaper change, brief snack, and daddy walking through the door. Then, it's back into the car seat to go home, see mommy, and then move through other routines and rituals of reconnection before the bedtime routines that signal the long separation of night sleep.

Routines lead to expected behavior *on both sides of the interaction.* In infants, we see something called "anticipatory calming." This is when, for example, the hungry baby calms as soon as mom makes "the right moves" that signal food is on the way. Baby is just as hungry, yet she has learned that there's no need to keep expressing her hunger because she trusts that the discomfort of hunger is about to go away. For the toddler who every morning gets breakfast just as soon as the overnight diaper is changed, there is not as strong a need to bring lots of energy to demanding food, because he is beginning to anticipate (because of repetition supported by mom and dad's verbal rehearsal of the routine) that food is coming.

Routines reduce stress. When expectation and experience match, trust is built and stress is reduced. The young child who begins to learn to expect that his call brings help has a lower stress level overall. High stress (which is much different than reasonable challenge) is associated with higher levels of cortisol, a stress hormone that can interfere with learning.

Routines support learning. Routines are patterns, and the brain is a pattern-seeking organ. By sorting sensory input—sight, sound, smell, feel, etc.—as well as emotional responses, the brain lays the foundation for learning. Later the brain will use the patterns developed from family, friends, and world experiences to structure and prioritize. Also, basic routines begin to be integrated or "chunked," freeing up more working memory to take in new information.

Routines can be fun. The cleanup song can make putting toys away a game—and it's more fun to turn the sock drawer into a basket and those rolled up pairs of socks into a basketball (and why not keep score and practice counting at the same time?).

Routines can and should change. Routines can begin to feel, well, routine. **The human brain seeks novelty; it's wired to get bored.** So when a valuable routine like the cleanup song becomes less pleasurable, it's a signal that the routine needs something new. Change it up or add a bit of challenge:

> *I'll pick up the blue toys, you pick up the red ones;*

> *Can you get all the cars into that bin, before I get all the blocks into this one?*

Notice that the underlying routine of cleanup did not change. The shift from *song* to *sorting* and *team play* or *race me* reflects the new abilities of a developing mind.

When expectation and experience match, trust is built and stress is reduced.

DEVELOPING ROUTINE AND RITUAL

You and your family will define the routines that work best for your family—just as there are households that do a load of wash a day and others that do multiple loads only on Sunday, the difference is one of style and workflow. The problem arises when there is no defined routine. That's when everyone wakes to discover no clean socks! Building your routines and rituals takes some thought. Here are some suggestions that may be helpful:

Consider how much time it takes

- Babies and toddlers cannot be hurried; give yourself an ample amount of time.

Build-in some back-up

- Babies and toddlers are unpredictable; Preparation can help.

- As a matter of self-defense, your routine should include a backup set of fresh clothes—for you too! Just-in-case garments hanging in your car can spare you the pressure of a disrupted routine. Also, wearing a robe over your work clothes may help with the inevitable spills and smears of the morning.

Follow the airline metaphor: "Secure your own oxygen mask before assisting others"

- For mornings, this often means getting up early enough to get yourself together before the rush of others and their various needs begin (as a benefit, having your own quiet moments before the rush can support your spirit).

- Be sure *you* are completely ready to walk out the door before you start readying others and before you say, "Let's go!" All the work that went into getting your child ready to walk out the door may be lost and the routine disrupted if you are off somewhere looking for your keys.

Involve the whole team

- Don't assume that someone else in your household will "know" the routine. **We often don't realize we have a frame of reference until we bump into someone else's**.

- Clear, *non-accusing* discussion openers can create a climate of mutual respect and allow everyone to communicate hopes regarding the flow of the day. For example:

  > *I'm feeling really harried by the time I get us packed into the car. Which part of the morning details would be most satisfying for you to manage?*

- As your children grow older, engage them in the process of preparation and in gathering the details of their lives.

- *Charts* with simple pictures will help children know what they need to do and, for older toddlers, what to bring (see example on p. 76).

- Toddlers still need your involvement to accomplish most tasks, but you can set the groundwork for future success by taking the time to walk them through a few routine tasks of their day.

Use the night before

- Pack lunches, snacks, diaper bags, and backpacks as part of the routine of dinner cleanup (after all, food and dishes are already in motion).

- Set out clothes so no one has to think too hard in the morning. Have two appropriate options and let your toddler know she can be in charge of choosing between the two (she can practice the challenging task of making a choice and also feel a sense of control).

- Have a designated place for backpacks, keys, and any other item that may create drama in your routine. Train yourself to scan this area as part of your own bedtime routine.

Make cleanup a part of young children's routines

- Have at least some toy storage that is easy for a toddler.

- Sing cleanup songs or play simple matching games to keep cleanup entertaining, and also support attention to the tasks.

- Remember that clean-up routines also lay the foundation for matching and grouping skills that will support reading and mathematics.

Include treasured moments in your routines

- We often plan most for the tasks we find challenging, like getting out the door or household chores. Sometimes in our hurry the love messages get lost. Especially in coming and going rituals, make space for treasured moments, be it a morning snuggle; a goodbye ritual such as a family hug; a kiss of blessing for each child and adult on their way; or possibly a mealtime ritual in which each person shares a thought about the day and listens as others share their thoughts.

Again, there's no need to adopt a structure that doesn't mesh with the personalities in your family. Nor, do routines have to be rigid. Remember, most of the time we only become aware of our routines when they are disrupted.

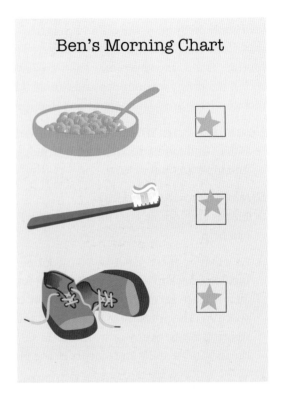

Ben's Morning Chart

Routines and rituals are powerful and important. Once established, they prime the child for what is coming next, easing how much you have to push and remind. They also plant the seeds of autopilot in preparation for more complex thinking skills.

And they build trust, as well as lifelong memories of family life.

CHORES WITH TINY PEOPLE

Children under 3 are natural collaborators. They want to please you and be with you.

When there is a toddler underfoot the day-to-day running of a household can seem like a Herculean task. But **what if instead of working around your toddler, your toddler worked with you?** Those little hands can be a big help. In fact, children under three are natural collaborators. Plus, toddler chores are good for child development, good for parents, and good for family too.

FIRST, SHIFT

To make this work it is helpful to first consider (and perhaps shift) your thinking. **There is a rather common mythology that only parents make a family work.** We may hear this reflected in language such as, *"my kitchen"* or *"my floors."*

In truth, everyone contributes. If you want your child to grow into a person who takes responsibility for doing his or her part, you have to believe that everyone in the family has a shared responsibility for making the family function.

Small people help is a different kind of help. If the mindset is "my child is helping me," then the frame of reference is "mine." But your child's help and the effort it takes you to monitor will look and feel different when the frame of reference shifts to the child.

By contributing in whatever small way, children can display and build competence, develop life skills, and internalize confidence and a sense of efficacy.

This is not about getting the child occupied so that you can get stuff done. Rather, together you are getting (some) stuff done as you teach and guide your toddler.

BENEFITS PACKAGE

For your toddler the benefits that come with this job include:

- Being with you

- Getting to say, "I did it!" (with much delight)

From Chores to College?

From matching-by-like, sorting-by-difference, identifying color, mixing, naming, and working with volume, a great deal of the academic curriculum is embedded in the day-to-day functioning of the family.

- Feeding the brain's hunger to learn
- Sowing the seeds for understanding math, science and other academic subjects.

Benefits for you include all of the above, plus a few to-dos checked off your list and, because you are not worrying what your toddler might be up to while you are busy, you get to give your third eye a rest.

SAFE PRACTICES

Safety is paramount! Cleaning solutions are off-limits, as are sharp surfaces.

Even if you are not using a toxic solution, be aware that you do not inadvertently tip off the child to where it is or how to override the safety lock (if you have one), as you collect cleaning supplies. To a child's eye, that blue and pink stuff can look like a child's drink, but instead be a "pretty poison."

SUPPLIES

Some existing tools can be sized down
- for instance, you can take the middle bar out of a Swiffer® sweeper.

Functional child-sized tools can also be purchased
- Child-sized rakes, brooms, and gardening supplies can now often be found in many stores.

- Day care suppliers are another source for child-sized tools, including specific cleaning supplies. Many of these suppliers can be found online.

But you needn't invest in special tools
- A sock over the hand works wonderfully

- Children love feather dusters

- A dry or slightly damp cloth, warm not hot, will do just fine, as will microfiber cloths that are made to be used without cleaners.

TIPS

- To a toddler everything is novel. Generally, they want to please you and be with you. They are curious and they delight in being helpful. **If you simply start the work, your toddler is likely to want to join in.**

- Do not ask (*"Do you want to...?"*). Instead, report:

  I'll wash the top windows, you wash the bottom ones.

- Keep your language about chores *positive* and also *inclusive*. They are not *your* windows, but *our* windows. He is not helping you with *your* work; you are *both* taking care of the family home.

- Save the complex chores (such as bill paying) and the too big and potentially dangerous work (such as lawn mowing) for a time when you are alone.

SAMPLE CHORES YOUNG CHILDREN CAN DO

On the next two pages, you'll find ideas for how toddlers can help with daily tasks such as grocery shopping, laundry, cleaning, and more. While we hope these suggestions are helpful, they are just a start. As you tend to the work of family and household, you will no doubt see many more ways your toddler can participate in a safe and encouraging way.

It may take some patience on your part, perhaps some adjustment in thinking, and, certainly, the chore will take longer and may not get done to your usual adult satisfaction, but by starting now, with a child that is not yet resistant, you are establishing a collaborative household over the long term.

Plus, even though the chore is small and short, **you may find that the companionship of working together has, in itself, lightened your load.**

GROCERY SHOPPING

- **Finding Groceries.** This can be done simply. For instance, if your child already knows what the cereal box or carrots look like ask him to point out those items on the shelf.

  Or, you can create a visual (but small) list that your child is in charge of by placing pictures on notecards and using a key ring to keep them together. When he points to a similar looking product, talk about what is similar and what is different (you are teaching, while also guiding him to the correct product).

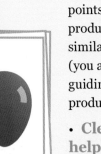

- **Clean hands can help put sturdy items away.** Open the crisper drawer and your child can put in the vegetables, same with the cheese drawer. Non-spillable dry goods can be put on low shelves, etc.

  Be aware that canned goods can be very heavy and easily dropped on small feet. Keep products light.

  Perhaps, your child can have a reusable grocery bag all her own. At checkout, put her favorite items and those that she will be able to put away inside of it. Have a special hook, where she can hang it up.

CLEANING

- **Dust smooth and easy to reach surfaces** with a damp cloth or old sock over the hand. You can draw a simple face on an old white sock for a puppet of Mr. Dusty.

Mr. Dusty

- **Wash windows with water**. Lint free and microfiber cloths make it easier for a child to wipe windows with fewer streaks. Teaching a child to be in charge of the fingerprints and pet marks on a sliding glass door is another chore well within their reach.

  [While there are natural and safe cleaning solutions, toddler fingers often go to the mouth and the eyes, and while a bit of vinegar may not harm, it could feel unpleasant—you will want associations with chores to remain positive.]

- You can build one more step after each bath or shower: Give your child a spray bottle with water and **have him rinse the tub/shower walls.** It is much easier to clean when soap scum has not been left behind. Later he can explore using squeegees.

WATER

MEAL PREPARATION

Many kids enjoy the science of food. If you are able to plan some extra time for food preparation, have them help **pour, stir, and mix.** The keys are: your patience, their clean hands, a safe step stool or high seat to keep your child at your eye level, and, in the case of mixing, oversized large bowls.

Food prep tasks are best saved for lunch, dinner, and snacks. Avoid asking much from your young child in the morning before they have had a chance to break the long nighttime fast.

Young children can help with food in many ways. For example, placing layers of vegetables in a bowl in preparation of the evening salad or shaping frozen bread dough for rolls can be both fun and great contributions to meals. Toddlers can also:

- **Carry non-breakables** to the table.

- **Set the table** (you can create paper placemats with outlines of the place setting so the child can match shapes, or with pictures so the child can match the image).

- Cooking-with-kids **books and web sites** can also help with ideas.

LAUNDRY

- **Sort clothes** by color before washing.

- Have the child **push the buttons** on the machine and then maybe go for a ride in the laundry basket.

- Find and **match socks** while folding.

- Even having children **separate clean laundry** into piles that go in each person's drawers will encourage an awareness of size and use.

DISHES

- **Wash and rinse** plasticware and other non-breakable items (add in some bubble play).

- **Help empty the dishwasher** by putting spoons away, or the non-breakable toddler plates and cups. You may have to reconsider where these items are stored to limit the climbing risks.

Too many toys can be overwhelming

Too many toys may be getting in the way of play. If your child takes many things out but does not really spend time playing with them, then it's probably time to pack up some and set them aside until you find the right amount for your little one.

The set-aside items can be reintroduced on a day when the weather will not allow you to be outside, or traded back in at another time.

MAINTAINING PLAY SPACE

Toddlerhood is the age of scattered toys and play equipment. It is often helpful to create a **simple ritual of pickup once or twice a day**, usually before a nap and as part of the bedtime routine.

Having **simple boxes or baskets** in which similar toys can be placed, and **playing matching games and racing games** as part of the process of clean up are just some of the engaging strategies parents have used to plant the seeds of responsibility.

SMALL PEOPLE IN BIG PLACES:
STORES, RESTAURANTS, & OTHER PUBLIC PLACES

EMPATHY—it's not pity, it's not assuming your understanding is the only one. Empathy is standing in another's shoes and seeing through another's eyes. It's acknowledging that their world looks and feels different than yours.

Spending time at home is lovely; feeling trapped at home is not. Unfortunately, isolation is a real risk for parents of young children. It can start early. When caring for an infant, the world beyond the front door can feel hard to manage. Along with various health and safety considerations, there's the potential for sudden-onset crying or lack of places to comfortably feed or breastfeed.

When baby begins to toddle, more challenges emerge. Stronger legs can run, stronger lungs can belt out a scream, and now there's that looming possibility of a public meltdown. Anyone can begin to think it's easier to just stay home.

But isolation is a risk factor for depression. Staying connected is essential. So is staying realistic.

Unreasonable standards, such as perfect behavior (whether from you or your child) can take a huge toll on self-esteem.

So, if you're feeling quarantined, remember that journeying out into the world—though imperfect and sometimes stressful—is good for you. And it's good for your child. Not only does your own well-being effect your toddler's well-being, the world offers your toddler a wonderful opportunity for learning.

Of course, some journeys will go better than others, but you probably already know how to increase the odds of a good day out and you will be figuring out more along the way.

You don't have to figure it out alone and you don't need to completely reinvent the wheel. Here, we offer you strategies. *Each* is illustrated within a specific public setting. Yet, *most* can be easily applied just about anywhere. And *all* come from the same source: *Empathy.*

In fact, empathy is the best source you will ever have for supporting anyone of any size. Empathy gives you different eyes, and when you focus those new eyes on places as familiar as, for example, the grocery store, you will gain insight into how to help your little one.

Is it just the wrong place?

Strategies can only help so much if the particular environment is not at all suited to your child.

In many areas, the neighborhood market has gone the way of the megastore. These are often noisy, brightly-lit, and can quickly stimulate the senses to the point of overload. Some children can manage this atmosphere, but many will find it overwhelming and upsetting.

Likewise, the slow pace of some restaurants is simply too much to ask of a body that needs to engage gross motor muscles every 3 to 5 minutes.

You can gauge your child's level of distress, as well as tolerance for reduced physical activity, and know to save certain trips for when you are able to leave your child in the care of someone else.

ON THE GO WITH TODDLER IN TOW

Most of us have an out-the-door checklist, though we may be barely aware as our inner manager checks off coat, keys, lightswitch, etc. When we become responsible for children, that checklist is longer and our inner manager needs the assistance of our more conscious self. So now before walking out that door we consider the structure of the day, the disposition of everyone, as well as the environment we will be entering. We ask questions such as:

> *Are we well-rested enough for this trip?*

> *Are we well-fed enough for this trip?*

And, because many of our social environments are challenging for children, we ask:

> *Do we have our helpful* [toy, blanket, etc.] *with us?*

And when we come to a "No" we problem solve. This could mean anything from bringing the stroller along to opting to save the trip for after lunch or another day altogether.

ON THE GO WITH A "SPRINTER" IN TOW

For some children, a wide-open space is an invitation to run, and a grocery or library aisle can look a lot like a sprinter's lane. But it is not socially acceptable, nor safe for others, to have a little sprinter in the book stacks. Also, it is too easy to lose visual track of a child in a mall or store aisle, and—of course—we all fear the most dangerous of all: a parking lot where even thoughtful drivers may miss seeing a small child in time to stop.

Anticipation + Planning= Prevention. There is nothing more likely to prevent child injury than adults who anticipate risk and plan for safety. If you know in your heart that every time your toddler is on his feet, running is likely, then you can create a safety plan.

For example, grocery parking lots become instantly safer when parents park near the cart racks and immediately transfer their potential sprinters from the car seat to the cart seat. Then, on return, either secure him in the car seat *before* unloading groceries or keep him strapped in the cart and engaged with you (see next paragraph) until all groceries are in. These precautions are especially important when you are also transferring another child, such as an infant.

Children go where their eyes lead. You may already be well aware of this fact—perhaps from watching infants climb headfirst down the stairs! We actively train children how to move through the world in a safe way. Because bodies follow eyes, when transferring to and from a car seat some toddlers can be kept safe through on-going eye contact and conversation. While this engagement can help, it is not full proof, and not enough of a precaution for high-active toddlers or distracted parents.

Actively teach safety. Although we need to remember that even elementary-age children are at risk of running into traffic (chasing after a ball, for instance), we still must teach basic safety rules and *provide supervised opportunities to practice them.* Before beginning to practice, you will talk about and point out examples of how young children hold hands with an adult when in a parking lot. Report to the child the way the world works:

> *Those big cars can't see you. I'm tall. They can see me. That's why you stay close to me.*

Then, at a time when everyone is rested and unhurried, you begin to practice. Some children will quickly want to "do it myself" and resist holding hands. If that is the

case, you will immediately carry her or place her in the stroller and tell her that she can practice another day.

If this triggers resistance or a meltdown, remember you are practicing when you have no other pressing agendas. If need be, you can return home.

There are, of course, variations. Some children may be happier having a parent hold their clothes rather than their hand, or, when they can, participate in pushing the cart with mom or dad to the entrance. Whatever variation, we must remain aware that toddlers cannot accurately anticipate the risk of injury to themselves or others. In other words, when out and about with young children, parents are always on safety duty.

THE QUICK EXIT

Sometime, somewhere you will have to leave suddenly and unexpectedly. This is just a fact of life. Though you may not be able to predict it, you can prepare for it with an escape valve. The most important aspects of an escape valve are:

- to have one, and

- to know what it is ahead of time so you are not scrambling to figure it out at the same time you are trying to calm your child.

There's no need for an elaborate plan. Having in mind a simple step or two is enough to help should things go haywire. On occasion, you are likely to find yourself at odds with various social conventions. Remember that in circumstances such as these *it really is okay* to switch your restaurant order to carry out or to leave your cart in the aisle. (Perishables in the cart? You can quickly inform someone on staff. They may even set it aside for your return.)

How should a toddler behave in a grocery store? Should he...

...stand up in the cart?

...grab cans and boxes from the shelf?

...run up and down the aisle?

No, of course not. This behavior is unsafe and inconsiderate. But it is also normal. Toddlers are developmentally driven to move and to use their muscles and every bodily sense to soak up information.

In the context of physiology, grabbing, standing and running are perfectly appropriate impulses. The toddler body wants and needs to be busy.

So when it has to be restricted, **give that trapped body something to do.**

- Older toddlers can push a child-sized cart.

- Younger ones can be strapped into the grocery cart but have a steering wheel to engage them.

- As always, amusements such as toys, books, even a key ring, can be a great help.

Toddlers also need attention, so much so, that it doesn't matter if that attention is positive or negative.

Sometimes children will simply enjoy experimenting with their voices, but they also know that screaming is a very good way to get mom or dad's eyes on them.

To avoid this happening be sure that as you focus on shopping, you also have some tools that support engagement for your little one.

For some, this can be as simple as a song or a well-timed ritual of kisses or rubbing noses. Or it may require a more involved activity, which can add in the extra benefits of learning and fun (and often will work best when you are not pressed for time).

ACTIVITIES FOR GROCERY STORE FUN

- Talk to your toddler about the foods she likes and where they are in the grocery store.

- If the grocery list is brief, use conversation to track what you have and what you have yet to find in the store.

- Make it a *treasure hunt*:

  Do you think our cereal is around this corner? Let's see...

- As children grow beyond eating or tearing paper, they can be the keeper of the grocery list or coupons. Not only does this give your child a focus, he now has some buy-in to this otherwise foreign activity.

- Create a *seek-and-find game* by cutting out labels or images of products you commonly purchase (for an example see p. 80). Arrange them on a child-safe ring or sturdy paper or cardboard and have your child tell you when she sees it in the store (learning to match pictures is one of the early literacy skills).

An activity that includes the child in the task at hand has benefits beyond meltdown prevention:

- It allows the child to feel like a contributing member of the family.

- It supports self-esteem, which is one-part capability (*Look what I can do!*) and another part loveablility (*Me and Mom together!*).

- It's also a great way to teach direction (up, down, middle) and color, as well as letter and image matching:

  > *The picture is of a purple box, do you see any purple?*

  > *That is purple, let's look closer, is it the same shade of purple?*

  > *No, oh, do you see another purple?*

  > *Over there? Yes, let's look...*

LOGICAL CONSEQUENCES

Connect the dots. Remember to (*matter-of-factly*) tie flavor rewards to behavior within the store:

> *Stores aren't for yelling. If you can find your inside voice we can stay and shop for your favorite strawberry yogurt. But if we need to, we will go home now, and then we won't have any strawberry yogurt in our refrigerator, and that will be sad.*

Want to Come Back? Make it Positive.

If you want your children to build a relationship with a place that is important to you, you will need to find people or things there that will leave your child with warm and happy associations.

Shushing and irritation, for instance, do not make a child feel she is in a place where she is loved and wanted.

Remember, small things matter. As Dr Yvonne once advised a congregation, "If you want toddlers to like being here, you have to change the brand of tissues. Toddlers do not like people to sandpaper their noses!" (and, really, who does?)

Restaurants demand two behaviors that are very challenging for young children:

 Be still   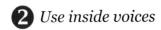 *Use inside voices*

It will help to practice these behaviors in an understanding environment ("family-friendly"). Many establishments advertise themselves as such, but some signs that little people are welcome include relatively quick service, a kid's menu, and good seating.

In some cases, good seating translates into a booth where, with your diligent supervision, a small child can stand and walk a few steps between a wall and you as the barrier. It may also mean a well-designed booster seat that is easy for both parent and child to manage.

Remember, an overstimulating environment may not be as family-friendly as advertised.

If the space seems too loud for your child, you may find it easier to order takeout and picnic at home until the child can better tolerate the sound intensity.

When more than one adult is available for support, it can sometimes be helpful to take the child for a walk after ordering. Whether back to the car for a few minutes or to the restroom to wash hands, a little journey helps minimize the amount of time the child must be still.

Usually you will want to have some supplies along. Some common restaurant tools are:

- **Busy boxes.** (these are often child size backpacks with appropriate toys designated for "travel times").

- **Emergency snack.** Young bodies can feel hunger intensely and waiting is not yet part of their skill set. In this context, it is okay to bring outside food into a restaurant.

- **Objects**, such as a small play vehicle, that engage both adults and children. Interaction through an object reinforces communication through eye contact and smiles, instead of voice. This can help to reduce yelling.

Though tools can help keep your toddler busy, they are unlikely to free you up for exclusive adult conversation. Remember, your engagement with your child will help keep him happy and will also encourage him to think about mealtime as a time for everyone to talk and interact.

Electronic Devices: Consider the Benefit-to-Cost Ratio

It can be tempting to hand your child your smartphone or other device for distraction or entertainment. These are very powerful tools and often effective for quieting busy children. If you choose to use one, be aware that overuse can encourage children to "remove themselves" from interaction with those around them. Throughout life, shared meal times create opportunity for building friendships and strengthening relationships with those around us.

PUTTING IT ALL TOGETHER

This book offers both a broad context for understanding parenting, children, and family, *and* concrete, detailed support for those concerns you need help with *right now*. Although focused on the toddler years, much of what you've read here will continue to support your parenting skills as children grow through preschool, elementary, and teen years.

Temperament and parenting styles will remain relevant, as will routines & rituals, and more. But it's also true that **our go-tos for communicating with toddlers are never lost.** Empathy, body language, *"when...then"*: These tools and others will work with your 5th grader, your young adult, even your partners and colleagues.

Additional age- or topic- specific resources will continue to be helpful in keeping parenting skills sharp. While, as we have said before, parenting is an art practiced by you, it is also a learned skill, and as you meet new challenges, remember that adults learn in stages, just as children do. In general, those stages look something like this:

Awareness. Sometimes it is triggered by a goal or the need for a solution, but the route to awareness is not always so direct. It may present as guilt or regret, such as in response to a negative autopilot pattern of yelling. Awareness is an important place to be if new patterns are to be learned. However, at this phase, be aware that there is a risk of focusing so much on failure that you overlook successes and cannot envision a positive future.

Consciously Competent. In this stage of learning people often report "I can do it if I really think about it." Learners have new content and are actively exploring change. There's awareness of the old behavior and related outcomes, yet also conscious attempts to use different words or behaviors. It can feel awkward or formulaic to be living through this learning stage. Support from others is a good defense against discouragement, and it's vital to resist the mindset "I'll never be able to do this," which is an invitation to stop growing as a parent.

Un-consciously Competent. At this third stage, a skill has been practiced enough to become fully integrated or automatic. With a new autopilot, the mind is free to be more creative. Although you may still use phrases or patterns very like the book or teacher suggested, you are now bringing your own words, humor, and mental flexibility to problem solving.

THE GOAL

So with all this growing and learning, what's the goal? It is not to be a perfect family. Nor is it to try to make every day a happy day.

> **The goal is to be a parent with leadership patterns that continue to support children's growth and development.**

In other words, you are laying the foundation for your children to become fully competent people in their own right. We hope to raise kids who are not only able to feed and dress themselves and manage the flow of their days, but who also come to more awareness of personal choices and their responsibility for the outcomes of those choices.

Those tasks are yet before you. As your family grows from toddlerhood, your preschooler will practice making choices, your elementary child will come to understand logical and natural consequences, and your teen will come to recognize personal life choices and social responsibility.

By having read this book and continuing to explore basic skills and knowledge, you are laying a solid foundation for those profound growth steps to come. You are on an amazing journey and our best wishes are with you always.

ACKNOWLEDGMENTS

Any good book is more than the words of the authors. It reflects a network of thought, experience, influence, and support much too wide to list in full. Yet, in addition to our families, there are many to whom we would like to extend a special thanks. Yvonne is grateful to Jean Illsley Clarke for helping to define a rich and satisfying career, the professors and friends at the Ohio State University who guided her professional transition from high school math teacher to parent educator; as well as the teams from Grant Medical Center and Riverside Methodist Hospital with whom she shared both grief and celebration working with families. She would especially like to acknowledge the families—all the moms, dads, grandparents, caregivers, and children from classes, support groups, and Parent Helpline calls—who through their struggles and questions not only helped to prioritize the content of this book, but who gave the gift of their trust. It is a privilege, both joyful and humbling, that she feels to this day.

For their thoughtful comments, both authors would also like to thank Anya Beaupre, Ann Dennis, Deanna Hall, Clare Matthias, Sandy McNabb, and Jacki Spangler, as well as literary agent Jill Marr of the Sandra Dykstra Agency. Thanks also to Jennifer George, Ted Hattemer, and Ellen Hoover for being especially generous with their expertise. And finally, we would like to express our gratitude to all those who recognized the benefit of parent education and who, with already full lives, stepped forward to offer support for the parenting program and for this project. You know who you are and we thank you.